Pre-Intermediate

Just Right

Jeremy Harmer
Ana Acevedo
Carol Lethaby

Student's Book

Marshall Cavendish
Education

Text acknowledgements

Track 56, 3 Reproduced by kind permission of Battersea Dogs and Cats Home; 4 Reproduced by kind permission of Friends of the Earth.

Photo acknowledgements

p.8 top to bottom ©Dimitris Legakis/Rex Features, ©Face Adrenalin, Bloukrans Bungy, South Africa used with kind permission, Kingda Ka, New Jersey, USA ©Six Flags Great Adventure, used with kind permission, ©Nigel French/Empics Sports Photo Agency, Bono ©Reuters/Corbis, Bob Marley ©Pictorial Press/Alamy, Catherine Zeta Jones ©Allstar Picture Library/Alamy, Kylie Minogue Anthony Harvey (50/50)/Empics; p.9 tl ©Eye Ubiquitous/Rex Features, tr ©Ken Welsh/Alamy; p.10 tl Peter Hendrie/Lonely Planet, tr ©Tibor Bognár/Corbis, bl ©Jane Sweeney/Lonely Planet, br ©Carol Polich/Lonely Planet; p.12 l ©Charles Sykes/Rex Features; p.13 ©Carol Polich/Lonely Planet; p.16 ©John Foxx/Alamy; p.19 tl ©Image100/Alamy, tr ©Patrick Frilet/Rex Features, bl ©Image Source/Alamy, bc ©Dan Duchars/ImageState/Alamy, br ©Press Portrait Service/Rex Features; p.20 l to r ©Vladimir Godnik/Alamy, ©Bill Lyons/Alamy, ©Blend Images/Alamy, ©Chris Willson/Alamy; p.22 l to r ©Charles Sykes/Rex Features, ©Rolf Bruderer/Corbis, ©B.D.V./Corbis; p.24 ©Lumina Films Limited, used with kind permission; p.27 ©Allstar Picture Library/Alamy; p.30 tr ©James D. Morgan/Rex Features, l ©MGM/Everett/Rex Features, br ©Reuters/Corbis; p.32 ©Mark Sykes/Alamy; p.33 and 34 ©Sipa Press/Rex Features; p.37 ©Goodshoot/Alam; p.47 ©Royter Snow/Images.com/Corbis; p.50 ©Stockbyte Gold/Alamy; p.51 ©Tom Stewart/Corbis; p.53 ©Comstock Images/Alamy; p.54 l to r ©Neil Egerton/Rex Features, ©Rex Features, ©Patrick Frilet/Rex Features, ©Wally Bauman/Alamy, inset ©Johnny Green/PA/Empics; p.56 ©Nick Hanna/Alamy; p,.57 ©Tom Stewart/Corbis; p.58 1 ©Mujo Korach/IBL/Rex Features, 2 ©Joe Pepler/Rex Features, 3 ©Rex Features, 4 ©Action Press/Rex Features, 5 ©oote boe/Alamy, 6 ©TNT Magazine/Alamy, 7 ©Ray Tang/Rex Features; p.60 left side t to b ©Royalty Free/Corbis, ©Claudia Kunin/Corbis, ©Goodshoot/Alamy, ©Blend Images/Alamy, right side tl ©Rodolfo Arpia/Alamy, tr ©Paul Springett/Up The Resolution/Alamy, bl ©Stockdisc Classic/Alamy, br ©Comstock Images/Alamy; p.62 t ©Tony Harrington/StockShot/Alamy, b ©Ron Chapple/Thinkstock/Alamy; p.65 ©Patrick Giardino/Corbis; p.66 t ©Sierakowski/Rex Features, b ©Randy Faris/Corbis; p.67 ©Karel Lorier/Alamy; p.69 ©Richard T. Nowitz/Phototake Inc./Alamy; p.71 a ©Sipa Press/Rex Features, b ©Lehtikuva Oy/Rex Features; p.74 t ©Corbis, b ©John Foxx/Alamy; p.80 t to b ©Bruce Benedict/Transtock Inc./Alamy, ©Warren Diggles/Alamy, ©Stockbyte Silver/Alamy, ©G. McLeod; p.86 ©Steve Thornton/Corbis; p.87 ©nagelestock.com /Alamy; p.88 ©Caroline Rippin; p.91 ©BananaStock/Alamy; p.94 l ©Hulton Archive/Getty Images, c ©Sutton-Hibbert/Rex Features, r ©Terje Pedersen/Rex Features; p.95 l ©Getty Images News/Getty Images, r ©Mark Witfield/Rex Features; p.101 tl ©Shout/Rex Features, tr ©Ingram Publishing/Alamy, bl ©Richard Cummins/Corbis, br ©Phototake Inc.Alamy; p.106 t l to r ©Rex Features, ©CSU Archive/Everett Collection/Rex Features, ©Roger-Viollet/Rex Features, ©Action Press/Rex Features, c l to r ©Everett Collection/Rex Features, ©Everett Collection/Rex Features, ©Time & Life Pictures/Getty, ©Everett Collection/Rex Features, bl ©Roger Viollet/Rex Features; p.108 ©Chen Su/Panorama Stock Photos Co Ltd/Alamy; p.109 ©BananaStock/Alamy; p.110 1 ©Chris Gascoigne/View Pictures Ltd/Alamy, 2 ©David Jones/PA/Empics, 3 ©Gareth Copley/PA/Empics, 4 ©Jon Edward Linden/Arcaid/Alamy; p.111 t to b ©Julian Makey/Rex Features, ©VSL/allOver Photography/Alamy, ©PA/Empics; p.114 t to b, ©Eye Ubiquitous/Rex Features, ©Action Press/Rex Features, ©Eye Ubiquitous/Rex Features, ©Kip Rano/Rex Features, ©Joe Sohm/Visions of America, LLC/Alamy, ©Sipa Press/Rex Features, ©Charles O'Rear/Corbis, ©Rex Features; p.115 ©Paul Almasy/Corbis; p.117 ©Grant Smith/View Pictures Ltd/Alamy; p.121 ©Comstock Images/Alamy; p.122 ©Stock Image/Pixland/Alamy; p.126 ©John Crall/Transtock Inc/Alamy; p.128 l ©Neale Haynes/Rex Features, r ©Buzz Pictures/Alamy; p.131 r ©Fortean Picture Library, l ©Not Known; p.136 ©Bill Ross/Corbis; p.139 ©Image100/Alamy; p.141 ©Nick Hanna/Alamy; p.144 ©Image100/Alamy.

The publishers would like to thank Sue Ruston.

Marshall Cavendish Education
119 Wardour Street
London W1F 0UW
www.mcelt.com/justright

Designed by Hart McLeod, Cambridge
Editorial development by ms foundry
Illustrations by Jo Taylor, Yane Christiansen, Francis Fung
Rory Walker, Valeryia Steadman, Tim Oliver

ISBN-13: 978-0-462-00736-6
ISBN-10: 0-462-00736-7

Printed and bound by Times Offset (M) Sdn. Bhd. Malaysia

Contents

UNIT 1

The world of English

Listening: about countries

1 Look at this map. What do the countries in red have in common?

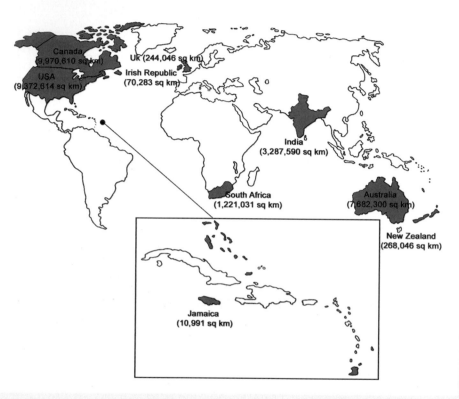

Canada
(9,970,610 sq km)

UK (244,046 sq km)

USA
(9,372,614 sq km)

Irish Republic
(70,283 sq km)

India
(3,287,590 sq km)

South Africa
(1,221,031 sq km)

Australia
(7,682,300 sq km)

New Zealand
(268,046 sq km)

Jamaica
(10,991 sq km)

Which 'red' country is the odd one out? Check your answer at the bottom of this page.

2 Look at the picture. Where are the people from?

Sandy   Matt   Wilson   Tessa

Listen to Track 1 to check your answer.

3 Who are the sentences about? Read the sentences. Then listen to Track 1 again. Who is each sentence about? The first one is done for you.

a He is from an island in the Caribbean. Wilson
b People in her country speak French or English, or both.
c Her city is bigger than the capital of her country.
d One in three families in his country speak English and another language.
e Reggae comes from his country.
f Eighty per cent of the people in his country live on the coast.
g Her country is in Great Britain but she is not English.
h His country is famous for its beaches and its mountains.

English is spoken as a mother tongue in all countries, except India. In India, English is an official language but not a mother tongue.

4 Read the text and listen to Track 2. Which word do you hear for each letter?

Hi! I'm Tessa, from Montreal, in Quebec. Quebec is in the (**a**) east/west/south of Canada. Most (**b**) people/Americans/Canadians speak the two official languages, French and English. Canada is a (**c**) big/huge/large country. The second largest country in the world actually. In Canada you can find (**d**) everything/anything/nothing. Do you like big (**e**) places/cities/countries? We have really exciting ones, like Montreal and Toronto. Do you like mountains? We have (**f**) two/lots/some too. (**g**) Water/Winter sports are very popular. It is very cold in winter, but I like summer better. It's warm and we go and swim in the lakes.

5 In pairs Guess the country.

Student A: go to **Activity 1 in the Activity Bank on page 134.**

Student B: go to **Activity 23 in the Activity Bank on page 140.**

Study grammar: comparative adjectives and adverbs

6 Copy the chart. Put the words in the correct columns.

beautiful fast high large popular
tall small sunny friendly

1 syllable e.g. big	2 syllables e.g. heavy	3 syllables e.g. Canada

Can you add more adjectives to the columns?

7 Look at these sentences. Then answer the questions.

New Zealand is big**ger than** Jamaica.
Jamaica is small**er than** New Zealand.
Mount Logan (Canada) is high**er than** Mount McKinley (Alaska, USA).
Jamaica is sunn**ier than** Scotland.
In Australia, Rugby is **more popular than** cricket.

a How do we make one-syllable adjectives into comparative adjectives?
b What happens when an adjective ends in a vowel + consonant?
c What happens when an adjective ends in 'y'?
d Why is 'popular' different?
e What word do we use after the comparative adjectives?

→ see 1A in the Mini-grammar

8 Look at the countries and the people in Activities 1 and 2. Complete the sentences and questions.

a New Zealand is .... (large) .... Jamaica.
b Matt is .... (young) .... Wilson.
c Is Wilson .... (friendly) .... Matt?
d Sandy looks .... (pretty) .... Tessa but Tessa looks .... (nice).
e Edinburgh is probably .... (beautiful) .... Glasgow but Glasgow is .... (interesting), Sandy thinks.
f Is Canada .... (big) .... the USA?
g Who do you think is .... (popular), Matt or Wilson? Tessa or Sandy?
h Canada is very cold in winter but it is .... (hot) .... England in the summer.
i Do you think people are .... (happy) when the sun is shining?

9 Look at the pictures and information on page 8. Make comparisons.

Examples: The Millennium Stadium is larger than the Edmonton stadium but it is smaller than Stadium Australia.

In Ireland, Bono is more famous than Kylie Minogue.

Large stadiums

Millennium Stadium, Cardiff, Wales	72,500 seats
Stadium Australia, Sydney, Australia	110,000 seats
Edmonton Stadium, Canada	60,000 seats

Mokai Canyon, New Zealand	80 m
Plettenberg Bay, South Africa	216 m
Pipeline Bungee, Australia	102 m

High Bungee Jumps

Tall roller coasters

Kingda Ka, New Jersey, USA	456 feet
Top Thrill Dragster, Cedar Point, Ohio, USA	420 feet
The Big One, Blackpool, England	235 feet

Australia: 1. Australian Rules football
2. Horse racing 3. Rugby League

Britain: 1. Football/soccer 2. Rugby 3. Cricket

USA: 1. Baseball 2. American football
3. Basketball

Popular sports on television

Famous people

Bono Ireland Catherine Zeta-Jones Wales Bob Marley Jamaica Kylie Minogue Austral

10 Think of special places and people in your country. Write comparisons.

Example: (In Brazil) I think Copacabana Beach is more famous than Ipanema.

11 Work out the comparative adverbs. Look at Activity 7 again. Then complete the sentences.

1 syllable
fast
hard

2 or more syllables
carefully
cheaply
easily
quickly

a Planes travel (fast) .... than trains.

b The traffic is terrible. You can probably get there (quickly) .... on foot than by car.

c You can travel (cheaply) .... in Jamaica .... in Canada.

d Dan drives (carefully) .... his sister.

e Sue had a map so she found the museum (easily) .... me.

f Tom worked (hard) .... Jim so he's taking a long holiday. Jim is staying at home.

Study functions: expressing preferences

12 Look at the photos. Which place is better for a holiday? Why? Make a note of your reasons.

13 Read the dialogue. Choose adjectives from the box to fill in the gaps. Make them comparative. You will not need them all.

> expensive   sunny   cheap   dry   exciting   relaxing

SONIA: So which is better, then, Fran? Marbella or Dublin?

FRAN: Marbella, definitely. It's more (**a**)............., and it's (**b**) ....! And it's got lovely beaches.

SONIA: But we always go to the beach. I'd rather do something different this year. Something more (**c**) .... Like a city. Like Dublin.

FRAN: There's a problem, then, Sonia.

SONIA: Oh? What's that?

FRAN: Because I like beaches. Well, I like beaches better than cities, anyway. And Marbella is (**d**) .... too. And it always rains in Ireland, you know, Sonia.

SONIA: No, it doesn't. And anyway, rain or no rain, there's more to do in Dublin.

FRAN: Like what? Museums and things like that? I'd rather stay here in London!

SONIA: OK then. You go to the beach and I'll go to Dublin. How's that?

FRAN: Oh, all right. You win. This time. But no museums, and no walking around in the rain.

Now listen to Track 3 and check your answers. What's the final decision?

14 Copy and complete the chart with phrases from the dialogue.

Asking about preferences	Expressing preferences
Which would you rather do?	I prefer cities to beaches.

What expression does Fran use to accept Sonia's preference?

15 Look at items a – f. Write down which you prefer. Give a reason.

a travelling on your own or travelling with a group
b travelling by bus or travelling by plane
c cities or beaches
d sunbathing or visiting museums
e sunshine or rain
f action holidays or relaxing holidays

Examples:

I'd rather travel in a group than travel on my own. It's safer.

I prefer travelling on my own to travelling with a group. It's easier.

I like travelling with a group better than travelling on my own. It's safer.

16 Compare your answers with other students. Do you agree? Are you good travelling companions?

Example:

STUDENT A: Which do you prefer, travelling on your own or travelling in a group?

STUDENT B: I like travelling with a group better. It's safer.

17 Role-play a conversation with your partner like the one in Activity 12. Choose two very different countries (one of them can be your own country if you want).

Reading: holiday postcards

18 Quick reading Read the postcards below and then answer these questions.

a When do people write postcards?
b Where are the people writing from?
c Who describes a place?
d Who describes some activities?
e Who describes people?

Dear Mum and Dad,
The flight was tiring and boring but here we are at last!
The Great Barrier Reef is huge – more than 2000 kilometres long! It's simply amazing. You can see lots of different (beautiful) fish, they say.
We are taking the train to Sydney on Tuesday. We will write again from there.
Love ya
Jessy

Hi everyone!
Montreal is beautiful! We went on a great city tour. We also took a boat ride on the Saint Lawrence River, but it's nicer to just sit at a street café and watch the world go by. Dad's disappointed because nobody can understand his French!
Take care!
Mum and Dad

Hi!
Cape Town is at the foot of Table Mountain. It's beautiful, modern and exciting. The beaches are great, and the nightlife is better! I am really excited because my dad was born here! Everyone is very friendly and we have met lots of interesting people.
I'm thinking of you all back home, cold and bored!
XXXX
Tricia

Hi guys!
We're staying on a ranch in Wyoming. There is absolutely nothing around here – it's the middle of NOWHERE! Every morning we get up really early and we go for a ride on the horses. Then it's breakfast and more riding – not my idea of fun! So today I walked to this little town to buy this postcard. Next week we go to San Francisco. I can't wait. I like cities better than the country!
Jerry

19 Take a closer look Find the answers to these questions.

a What is one of the languages people speak in Montreal?
b Who is not having a good time?
c Who did not enjoy their journey?
d Which city is at the foot of a mountain?
e Where are there no big towns?
f Which city will Jessy go to next?
g Whose family comes from the place she is visiting?

20 True [T] or False [F]?

a You can swim in Cape Town.
b Wyoming is a big city.
c Jerry likes big cities.
d The Great Barrier Reef is an ocean.
e The Saint Lawrence River is in Quebec.
f Table Mountain is near Sydney.

Study grammar: –ing and –ed adjectives

21 Listen to Track 4. Choose which words the speakers use.

GIRL 1: Let's do something. I am so boring/bored.

GIRL 2: No. You're quite good fun, really. But I'm bored too. Let's go out.

MAN: I'm going to watch this DVD about Jamaica. Are you interesting/interested?

WOMAN: Not very. But I am interesting/interested in the video.

MAN: You can't come with us? Oh I'm really disappointing/disappointed.

WOMAN: I'm disappointing/disappointed too. Next time, maybe.

What mistake are the first speakers making?

Which sentences are true about you?

a I am interesting.
b I am exciting.
c I am interested in music.
d I am disappointing.
e I am excited about other countries.
f I am boring.
g I am bored.

22 Read the explanations about adjectives. Then do the exercise.

Adjectives ending in '-ed'	Adjectives ending in '-ing'
describe how someone feels e.g. *Tricia is **excited** about Cape Town.*	describe the thing or person that produces those feelings e.g. *Tricia thinks Cape Town is **exciting**.*

→ see 1B in the Mini-grammar

Choose the correct adjective for each blank. Does it end in –*ed* or –*ing*? The first one is done for you.

a I find swimming very ...*relaxing*... (relax).
b Learning about other cultures is very .... (interest).
c I am .... (interest) in travelling.
d Jude was very .... (tire) after the long trip.
e Sharon thinks flying is .... (tire).
f The plane moved up and down but all the people were completely .... (relax).
g I was .... (worry) about the long flight.
h James finds my accent .... (amuse).
i The film was very .... (amuse). I laughed a lot.

23 **In pairs** Take turns to read the facts about the English-speaking world to your partner. React to the facts: use adjectives from the box.

Example: STUDENT A: One in five Canadians speaks French as a first language and learns English at school.

STUDENT B: Really? That's surprising. / I'm surprised.

amusing/amused   shocked/shocking   exciting/excited
interesting/interested   surprised/surprising

a One in five Canadians speaks French as a first language and learns English at school.
b Over 300 million people speak English as their mother tongue.
c About eighty percent of Australians live in cities and towns along the coasts.
d English is an official language in India and about 3,000 newspapers are published in English.
e Snow covers most of Canada from November until April.
f There are so many varieties of mangoes in Jamaica that they have run out of names. They now just number them.

24 Write a list of five things about your country.

Read the facts to your partner. How does he/she react?

Write about (a) things that interest you, (b) something that is interesting, (c) something that amuses or surprises you, or (d) something that is shocking/surprising/exciting.

Example: STUDENT A: In the south of Mexico, there is a language without words, just whistles.

STUDENT B: Really? That's interesting.

Study vocabulary: two-word nouns

25 Match the words in the left-hand column with their 'other half' in the right-hand column. The first one is done for you.

car cash	(office) station (x2)
police bus	mall agent
travel petrol	stop hire
(post) shopping	dispenser

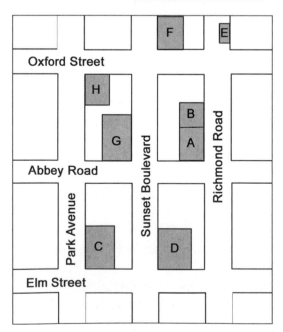

Oxford Street

Abbey Road

Elm Street

Park Avenue

Sunset Boulevard

Richmond Road

Choose a letter for each place (e.g. 'h – post office). Don't tell your partner. Ask your partner about their place.

Example: A: Where's the post office?

B: It's on Oxford Street, on the corner with Park Avenue.

HOLLYWOOD

26 Make two-word nouns for the following items.

Example: a station in the subway system – a subway station.

a A book with useful phrases in a foreign language.
b A room in a hotel.
c A hat to keep off the sun.
d Glasses to protect you from the sun.
e A calculator that you can put in your pocket.
f A bag for sleeping in.
g A book to guide you on your trip.
h A camera to make a video.

27 You are going to visit Hollywood, California, in the USA. Which of the items in Activity 27 do you need? Why? Tell your partner.

Example: I think I need a phrase book because my English is not very good.

Pronunciation: stress in two-word nouns

28 Listen to Track 5. Which stress pattern do you hear?

a <u>bus</u> stop   bus <u>stop</u>
b <u>city</u> map   city <u>map</u>
c <u>sun</u> hat   sun <u>hat</u>
d <u>post</u> office   post <u>office</u>

29 Mark the stress in these two-word nouns. Then listen to Track 6 and check your answers.

a sun glasses   e ski resort
b guide book   f hotel room
c subway station   g police station
d cash dispenser

30 In pairs Add a place…

STUDENT A: I went to the post office.
STUDENT B: I went to the post office and to the police station.
STUDENT A: I went to the post office, to the police station and to …'

How many words from Activities 25 and 29 can you add – and remember?

Writing: postcards

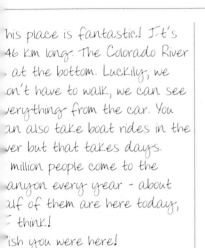

his place is fantastic! It's
46 km long. The Colorado River
 at the bottom. Luckily, we
on't have to walk, we can see
verything from the car. You
an also take boat rides in the
ver but that takes days.
 million people come to the
anyon every year – about
alf of them are here today,
 think!
ish you were here!
ruce

31 Look at the picture and read the postcard. Can you guess where it is from?

32 Which things are included in the postcard?

a Bruce's address
b information about the Canyon
c Bruce's opinion of the Canyon
d the date
e a greeting
f a signature

33 Answer the questions. Give your opinion.

Why didn't Bruce write his address and the date?
Why didn't he start the postcard with Dear…?
How does he end the postcard? Why?

34 Think of a place in your country. Write a postcard to an English-speaking friend. Follow the postcard style. Then 'send' the postcard to someone in the class. Can they guess where the postcard is from?

Speaking: which country?

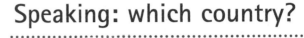

35 The situation: You want to go on holiday to an English-speaking country.

The problem: you have to find at least two people to travel with.

a Choose one of the countries on page 6. Write a list of your reasons for going there and what you want to do there.
b Talk to other people in the class about your preferences. Try to find at least two people to go on holiday with you.
c When you find two people to go with you, tell your teacher. Who can find two travelling companions first? Which country is the most popular?

UNIT 2
Don't get stressed out!

Listening: telling jokes

1 Read the jokes. Are they funny?

A – Waiter! Your fingers are in my soup.

– Don't worry Madam. It's not hot.

B – Knock, knock.
– Who's there?
– Boo.
– Boo who?
– Don't cry. It's only a joke!

C – Doctor, doctor. I keep seeing green hairy monsters with horrible faces.
– Have you seen a psychologist?
– No, just green hairy monsters with horrible faces.

D – Teacher: Jane, if you have ten sweets and Oscar asks you for one and Jackie asks you for two, how many sweets do you have left?
– Jane: Ten!

2 Can you guess the end (the punch line) of the cartoon?

Now listen to Track 7 and check your answer. Did you get the joke?

3 Listen to Track 8. Complete Sam's explanation.

SAM: The control tower wants his (**a**) .... and his (**b**) .... , right? As in 30,000 (**c**) .... But the pilot (**d**) .... height as in 'How (**e**) .... are you?' And the position as in 'Are you (**f**) .... or standing?' Geddit?

CLAIRE: Yeah, duh! But it's not funny.

SAM: OK, but I've got another one. Listen. There's this (**g**) .... and she comes into (**h**) ....

CLAIRE: Not (**i**) .... , Sam. I've got (**j**) .... to do.

4 Answer the questions. Listen to Track 8 again if you want.

a Why is Claire stressed out?
b Why does Sam tell her a joke?
c Is Claire less stressed now?
d Do you think laughter is a good thing when you are stressed?
e Claire did not find the joke funny. Did you?

5 In pairs Telling jokes.

Student A: go to **Activity 2** in the Activity Bank on page 134. Tell your partner the joke. Does he/she think it's funny?

Student B: go to **Activity 24** in the Activity Bank on page 140. Tell your partner the joke. Does he/she think it's funny?

Reading: stress

6 Check how stressed you are.

a Choose a phrase from the box to complete each sentence. Put the verb in the right tense.

> To have bad dreams   To feel angry or nervous
> To have headaches   To forget things   To sweat a lot
> To have a stomachache

1 He is having a bad dream

2 She ....

3 He ....

4 She often ....

5 He is feeling hot and
....

6 She ....

b Do you ever feel like the people in the pictures? Write sentences.

Example: I never/sometimes/often have bad dreams.

7 Answer the questions. Then compare your answers with your partner.

a How do people sometimes feel when they are stressed?

b What kind of things can give you stress?

c Is stress always bad for you?

8 Read these dictionary definitions. Look quickly at the text in Activity 9 on page 16. Which meaning (1 or 2) is the text about?

> **Stress /stress/ n 1** the feeling of being worried because of problems in your life. **2** special force we put onto a word or part of a word.

> **Just learning:** *predicting*
> Before you read a text, look at it. Where does it come from (newspaper, magazine, etc.)? What kind of text is it (article, poem, letter, email, etc.)? What do you expect?
> Now think about the topic (holidays, cars, stress, etc.). What do you know about the topic? What do you expect?
> Now you are ready to read the text!

9 Quick reading Read the leaflet. Answer the questions as you read.

Stress: the facts

Do you ever feel that you don't know what to do because there are too many things in your life? Then, you probably feel stress. Things that cause stress are called 'stressors'. One important stressor is change. For example, going to a new school or starting a new job can give you stress. Other common stressors are taking a test or being ill. But some stress can be good. For example, before a race most athletes feel nervous. This stress helps them get ready.

What makes stress good or bad? Let's look at an example: Jack has a new job in another city. He and his wife are very excited. But their children are sad to leave their family and friends. The move to another city is a good stressor for the parents but a bad one for the children. The parents and the children have different feelings about the situation.

When you are feeling stressed, these tips can help you:

• Eat lots of fruit and vegetables and meat and fish without fat. Salad is good too. Don't eat any snacks, like crisps, and don't drink any caffeine. Don't eat too much sugar – put the chocolate and cakes away.

• Do exercise everyday. Laugh! Make time for fun.

• Talk about your problems.

> Think about changes in your life. Did they cause you stress?

> Can you think of a time when stress helped you get ready?

> What is a good stressor for you? What is a bad one?

> What do you do when you are stressed? Do you use any of the tips?

10 Take a closer look Find the information in the leaflet.

a a definition of stress
b a definition of 'stressor'
c an important stressor
d things that can make stress good or bad
e some things that can make you feel better
f food that is bad for you when you are stressed

11 Look at your answers in Activity 7. Did you learn anything new about stress? What? Tell your partner.

12 Do you feel stress in the same way that other people do?

Compare your answers to the questions in the leaflet.

Example: STUDENT A: *Think about changes in your life. Did they cause you stress?*

STUDENT B: *I changed schools last year but I didn't feel any stress.*

Study grammar: countable and uncountable nouns

13 Copy and complete the chart with the nouns in the sentences.

Countable nouns (C)	*a potato – three potatoes*
Uncountable nouns (U)	*milk*
Countable and uncountable	*coffee – a coffee - coffees*

a Vegetarians don't eat <u>meat</u>.
b I had <u>fish</u> for lunch.
c Oranges, apples and bananas are all <u>fruit</u>.
d I love tropical <u>fruits</u>.
e <u>Sugar</u> is bad for you.
f <u>Crisps</u> have a lot of <u>salt</u>.
g Is <u>stress</u> a serious <u>problem</u>?
h I bought <u>salad</u> and a box of <u>chocolates</u>.
i There is a wide variety of <u>salads</u> in this cafeteria.
j I love <u>chocolate</u>. I bought a box of <u>chocolates</u>.

14 Study the chart in Activity 13. Choose the correct alternative.

a These nouns have a plural form.
Countable/uncountable

b You can't use numbers with these nouns.
Countable/uncountable

c You use 'a/an' with these nouns.
Countable/uncountable

d You can't use 'a/an' with these nouns.
Countable/uncountable

e These nouns are not normally used in the plural.
Countable/uncountable

→ see 6B in the Mini-grammar

15 Copy and complete this chart. Then compare your chart with your partner. Whose diet is the healthiest?

My typical diet
breakfast *eggs*
lunch
dinner
snacks

Study vocabulary: phrases with uncountable nouns

16 Make phrases using the uncountable nouns from the box with the amounts and containers in the pictures. Some of the nouns can be used with more than one amount or container.
Use the phrase a .... of ....

Example: *a jug of milk*

bread   cake
cereal   cheese
lemon juice
milk   oil   salt
soup   sugar   water

bowl

slice

cup

drop

jug

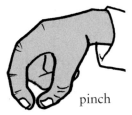
pinch

spoon

glass

How many phrases did you write? Compare them with your partner.

17 Guess the mystery word We can use the same word with all the following uncountable nouns in the phrase 'a .... of ....'. Use the clues to try to guess what word it is.

furniture   homework   advice   information   clothing   news

Clues
a You use this word to talk about a quantity of bread. (Can't guess? Try the next clue.)
b You also use this word to talk about a sheet of paper.
c You also use this word to talk about a portion of cake.
d Still can't guess? Unscramble the letters: EECPI.

18 Copy and complete the sentences. Use the mystery word and the nouns in Activity 17.

a How many .... of .... did you do for English last week?
b You won a prize? That's a great .... of ....!
c That table is a lovely .... of ....
d You feel stressed? Let me give you a .... of ....: relax a bit.
e The report is almost finished. We just need one more .... of ....
f A shirt is a .... of ...., usually for men.

Study grammar: talking about quantities

19 Look at the pictures and listen to Track 9. Can you make the recipe? Why (not)?

20 Listen to Track 9 again. Write the quantities for the recipe.

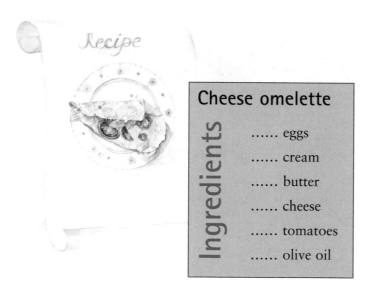

Cheese omelette

Ingredients

...... eggs

...... cream

...... butter

...... cheese

...... tomatoes

...... olive oil

Compare your answers with your partner.

21 Match the columns. The first one is done for you.

A little ———>	30 grams of butter
A few	24 eggs
Lots of	0 millilitres of milk
A lot of	4 tomatoes
No	1 kilo of cheese
No	0 potatoes

22 Copy and complete the chart with phrases from Activity 21.

	Countable nouns	Uncountable nouns
Large quantities	lots of a lot of many	lots of
Small quantities	some not many	not much
No quantity	no not any	no not any

→ see 6C in the Mini-grammar

23 Complete the sentences with as many words and phrases from the chart as possible.

a This hot chocolate is very, very sweet so don't put .... sugar in it.

b I love that shop. They have .... great cakes.

c .... people are learning to cook these days.

d This dish has .... butter and .... cream at all.

e .... recipes from this book, about three, are from India.

f .... people know this recipe, only some people in my family.

g Is there .... milk? I don't like black coffee.

h Are there .... cookies? I'd like some with my tea.

24 Complete the sentences with phrases from the chart in Activity 22.

a For this recipe you need .... tomatoes, not .... , just two or three.

b You also need .... chicken, say 200 grams.

c Then you need .... olive oil. Not .... , about two tablespoons.

d Next, you need .... bread – two slices.

e .... salad is nice – a leaf or two.

f You can also add .... cheese. Just .... small pieces.

Can you guess what the recipe is? Check your guess at the bottom of page 19.

25 In pairs What's your favourite easy dish? Tell your partner the ingredients you need for it.

Example: My favourite dish is rice with chicken. You need...

Study functions: asking for and giving advice

massage

oils

eyes   gym

sheep

26 Listen to Track 10 and put the pictures in the right order.

Put words in the gaps (you can use the words more than once).

LISA: What's up, Maggie?

MAGGIE: Uh? Oh, I need to relax. Got any ideas?

LISA: Yes. Try exercise.

MAGGIE: Exercise?

LISA: Yeah. Go to a (**a**) .... or something.

MAGGIE: No thanks. I don't like exercise.

LISA: OK, then. How about aromatherapy?

MAGGIE: What's that exactly?

LISA: It's a mixture of (**b**) .... and smells and (**c**) .... Very, very relaxing.

MAGGIE: Massage? That's not for me, I'm afraid.

LISA: You ARE difficult Maggie.

MAGGIE: Sorry!

LISA: I know. You can close your (**d**) .... and count (**e**) .... Slowly.

MAGGIE: How many (**f**) .... ?

LISA: You could count up to, say, 33,781.

MAGGIE: 33,7... .

LISA: Maggie? Maggie ... ha ha

Listen to Track 10 again and check your answers.

27 Listen to Track 10 again. Cover the dialogue in Activity 26 with a piece of paper. Which phrases in this chart can you hear in the conversation?

Asking for advice	Giving advice
Can you give me some advice?	Try ... .
	How about ...?
Got any ideas?	
	You can ... .
What can I do to ...?	
	You could ... .

28 Give Maggie some advice to help her relax. Use the phrases from the chart in Activity 27.

Example: *Don't eat too much at night. That's my advice!*

a have a cup of warm milk before bed
b do not eat too much at night
c do not watch television in bed
d listen to some relaxing music
e have a long warm bath
f go for a short walk

Can you think of more advice?

29 What can you advise these people to do?

a Samir can't concentrate on his work.
b Larissa always feels tired.
c Tom wants to look cool.
d Meena wants to lose weight.

Writing: *because, but, so*

30 Read these problems from students of English. Write down the problems that you have, too.

'I get stressed when I read in English because there are many words I don't know.' *Boris, Moscow, Russia*

'Sometimes I can't do the grammar exercises, so I get stressed.' *Amel, Cairo, Egypt*

'I like to speak in English, but I worry about my pronunciation.' *Feçir, Ankara, Turkey*

'I want to learn lots of words, but I don't know how.' *Koji, Nagoya, Japan*

31 Answer the questions. Write the words that helped you answer.

a Boris gets stressed – what is the reason? (because)

b Amel can't do the grammar exercises – what is the result of this?

c Feçir likes to speak English – what is the problem?

d Koji wants to learn new words – what is the problem?

32 Complete the sentences with *because*, *but* or *so*.

a There are many words I don't know, ... I can use a dictionary.

b I write down new words, ... I can look at them again and remember them.

c I want to learn English .... it is important for many jobs.

d English is sometimes difficult, ... I like it.

e I like having a workbook .... it has a lot of exercises.

f Sometimes I don't understand, ... I can ask my teacher for help.

33 In pairs Is learning English stressful? Some people think so! Can you help them? Write a leaflet with advice.

a Think quickly of ideas to make learning English easier and more enjoyable. Write them all down quickly, as you think of them.

b Choose 6 – 8 ideas you like best.

c Copy and complete the leaflet, using your ideas.

Take the stress out of learning English!

Why is learning English a good idea?

➠
➠
➠

Things about English that can be stressful.

➠
➠
➠

Things you can do to help yourself.

➠
➠
➠

34 Swap your leaflets with another pair. What do you think of the other pair's leaflet? How can they make it better?

Pronunciation: word stress

35 Listen to Track 11. Listen to these two-syllable words and look at their 'shapes'.

boring   tired   people

advice   excuse   repeat

36 Listen to Track 12. Match the words and the shapes.

a explain

b healthy

c accept

d diet

e massage

f lifestyle

g problem

h complete

37 Listen again and repeat the words.

38 Read these words. Which shape are they? Compare your answers with your partner.

a offer	b compare
c nervous	d amuse
e feeling	f topic
g alert	h relax

Listen to Track 13. Check your answers.

Speaking: role-play (advice)

39 You got a nice sum of money for your birthday and you got your first cheque at work. You can spend the money carefully or you can go crazy and spend it all. Copy and complete the chart.

I can spend the money on fun things:
Buy a new MP3.

I can spend the money carefully:
Put some of the money in the bank.

40 Get some advice

a Get advice from three different people. Choose the best advice.

Example: I don't know what to do with my money. Can you give me some advice?

b Tell your partner what you are going to do. Does he/she agree?

UNIT 3
TV and the media

Reading: do the media decide?

1 Look at the photos. Answer the questions.

a Would you like to look like these people?

b Would you like to live in a house like this?

c Would you like to have this kind of life?

a **In pairs** Ask about questions a, b and c.

Example: Did you answer 'yes' to question a? – Yes, I did. So you want to be thin? – Yes, and rich!

2 **Quick reading** What is the article about?

Are the media a bad influence?

Kirsty is fifteen years old. She likes doing what every other girl her age enjoys. She goes to school, she watches TV and goes shopping with her friends. But Kirsty has an ambition: she wants to be a model. Every week, she saves her pocket money to buy magazines. She studies the photos of famous models. They are her role models. Kirsty's mother, Stella, is not happy. 'It's OK to have ambitions,' she says. 'But in Kirsty's case it's becoming an obsession. She thinks about it all the time.' According to Stella, Kirsty does not have a healthy diet and she exercises more than normal because she wants to be thin. She worries that Kirsty is developing an eating disorder. 'The media are responsible for this situation,' her mum says. 'All the teen magazines and teen programmes on TV tell children that the only important thing is how you look – your appearance. They say 'you want to be happy? Then be thin!'
Are the media really responsible for situations like Kirsty's? Kirsty's big sister Donna, 18, disagrees. 'I buy lots of magazines but I don't want to be like the people in them.' says Donna. 'Magazines show you all kinds of people, not just celebrities. They give information and have nice pictures. That's why I like them.'
So, who is right? Do the media decide how we look and how we live? Are we all becoming obsessed with celebrities and their lifestyles?

b **Discussion** Do magazines and TV programmes control your life?

a the influence of media on people's lives
b a girl who wants to be a model
c popular magazines
d two sisters?

> **Just learning:**
> *skimming*
> When you want to find out what a reading text is about – when you just want to get the 'general idea' – don't read every single word in detail. Just read the text quickly to understand the main idea (you can worry about the details later). Reading like this (for quick general understanding) is called skimming.

3   Take a closer look.

Why …

  a   does Kirsty buy magazines?
  b   does Donna like magazines?

How …

  a   does Kirsty keep thin?
  b   does Stella feel about Kirsty?

What …

  a   docs Stella think about the media?
  b   does she think about having ambitions?

4   Vocabulary Find words in blue in the text which mean:

  a   You want to copy these people because you think they are fantastic.
  b   Parents give their children this money to spend.
  c   Something you can't stop thinking about – all the time!
  d   You have this when you really want to do well.
  e   The power to change what people think or do.
  f   A medical problem – you don't eat normally.
  g   You are this when you are the cause of something or the reason for something.

5   Answer the questions in the article.

  a   Are the media a bad influence?
  b   Are the media really responsible for situations like Kirsty's?
  c   Do the media decide how we look and how we live?
  d   Are we all becoming obsessed with celebrities and their lifestyles?

Compare your answers with your partner.

Study vocabulary: reading, watching, listening

6   Match the columns. You can use the verbs more than once.

Read …	a comic	the news
Watch …	a magazine	an article
Listen to …	a newspaper	a report
	a programme	the weather forecast

7   Match the definitions a – h with the shows.

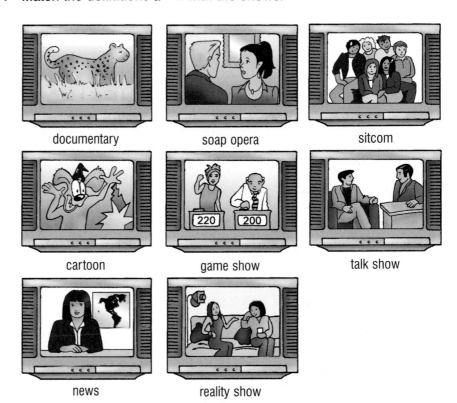

documentary   soap opera   sitcom

cartoon   game show   talk show

news   reality show

  a   a radio or television story about the lives of a group of people. It's on almost every day and doesn't have an end. It's usually very dramatic/exciting.

  b   a radio or television programme that gives people information, every day, about things that are happening in the world

  c   a competition on radio or television – people win prizes

  d   a programme with real people, not actors

  e   a programme with facts and information about nature, historical events or science

  f   a presenter invites famous people to the studio and they talk about different things

  g   a funny story each week about the same group of people. They are usually in the same place.

  h   adventures and funny stories, made with drawings and pictures – not real people and scenery

8 Copy and complete the chart with words from the box. You can use the words more than once.

> programme station channel article
> presenter headline journalist reporter
> newsreader disc jockey (DJ)

THE MEDIA	RELATED WORDS
radio	
television	
newspapers and magazines	*headline*

9 **In pairs** Tell your partner the name of a programme. They say what type of programme it is.

Example: STUDENT A: *The Simpsons*

STUDENT B: *It's a cartoon*

Study grammar: the present simple

10 Read the sentences. Which verbs are in the present simple?

a She goes to school, she watches TV and goes shopping with her friends but she doesn't eat well.
b In game shows people play games or answer questions and win prizes.
c Most people buy magazines and watch TV.
d Why do people like reality TV?
e In the famous novel *Jane Eyre* (1847), Jane marries Mr Rochester.

11 Copy the chart. Complete it with the sentences in Activity 10.

We use the present simple to ...	Examples
... talk/ask about repeated actions and habits	
... talk/ask about general facts which are true and will be for some time	
... describe what happens in a film, book, television or radio programme	

→ see 10A in the Mini-grammar

12 Choose the correct form of the underlined verbs to fill in the blanks.

a I <u>cry</u> when I watch soaps. My mother .... too.
b I <u>buy</u> magazines once a month but my sister .... them every week.
c My parents <u>watch</u> the news every night. My brother often .... with them.
d In my house nobody <u>reads</u> the papers during the week but we all .... them at the weekend.
e We <u>don't have</u> a college newspaper. My friend's college .... one either. Maybe we can start one.
f Our neighbours <u>have</u> many TV channels but we .... only five.
g We <u>have</u> a DVD recorder so I usually <u>record</u> my favourite documentaries. My grandmother .... one so I sometimes .... programmes for her.

13 Think of a TV or radio programme. Write true sentences about it.

Who are the main characters/participants?

Acerola and Laranjinha. They are young men. They live in Rio de Janeiro, in Brazil.

What is the programme about?

The life of people in big cities.

When is it on?

Saturday at 9 o'clock.

14 **In pairs** Ask and answer questions about the information in your charts in Activity 13. DO NOT SAY the name of the programme.

How quickly can you guess the name of the programme? Write down the number of questions you ask.

Example: STUDENT A: *Who are the main characters?*

STUDENT B: *The two main characters are Acerola and Laranjinha.*

STUDENT A: *What is the programme about?*

STUDENT B: *About poor people in big cities.*

15 **Complete the questions.**

a What .... Kirsty .... to be? She wants to be a model.

b What .... your younger sister .... with her pocket money? She buys books.

c .... don't some girls .... well? Because they want to be thin.

d .... some people want to be thin? Because they want to look like the models in magazines.

e .... you .... TV? Every evening after dinner.

f .... you .... listening to the radio? I love it! I can't do anything without music.

Listening: street survey

16 Listen to Track 14. What is the survey about? Write down any words that helped you decide.

17 Listen to Track 14 again. How does each person answer the questions?

Television: people's preferences

Age: 26   Sex: **Male**

Q1: How many hours a day do you watch television?
☐ 2 – 4 hours ☐ 4 – 6 hours
☐ more than 6 hours

Q2: What kind of programmes do you prefer to watch?
☐ news ☐ soap operas
☐ documentaries ☐ game shows
☐ sitcoms ☐ sport

Q3: Do you watch other kinds of programmes?
☐ No
☐ Yes (say what) ....

Television: people's preferences

Age: 19   Sex: **Female**

Q1: How many hours a day do you watch television?
☐ 2 – 4 hours ☐ 4 – 6 hours
☐ more than 6 hours

Q2: What kind of programmes do you prefer to watch?
☐ news ☐ soap operas
☐ documentaries ☐ game shows
☐ sitcoms ☐ sport

Q3: Do you watch other kinds of programmes?
☐ No
☐ Yes (say what) ....

18 Listen to Track 14 again. How did each person answer the following question?

Why do you watch television – for information or for fun?

Which of the people do you agree with? Why?

19 Copy the questionnaire in Activity 17. Use it to interview other people in the class.

Writing: survey report

20 Read the survey report and answer the questions.

TELEVISION: SURVEY REPORT

Sample: 240 people between the ages of 18 and 35 were interviewed.

1 Hours spent watching television
70% of people asked watch 4-6 hours
25% watch 2-4 hours
5% watch less than two hours

2 Preferences
45% of people asked prefer sitcoms to any other programme
35% prefer soap operas
15% prefer documentaries
5% prefer news programmes

3 Reasons for watching TV
75% of people asked watch for entertainment
18% watch for information
7% watch to learn new things (for educational purposes)

Conclusion: Most people watch between 4-6 hours every day. Sitcoms are the most popular programme in this age group. Most people watch television for entertainment. Few of the people in this age group are interested in the news.

a How many people answered questions?
b How old were they?
c How many people watch TV for more than 4 hours a day?
d What kind of programme do most people watch?
e Are there any people who watch TV to learn new things?

21 Using information from your survey in Activity 19, write a report about the people you interviewed. Present your report to the class. Is your conclusion the same as the report in Activity 20?

Study grammar: present simple, subject and object questions

22 Look at the pairs of questions. Say what is different about them.

a 1 Who does Kenny admire?
  2 Who admires Kenny?

b 1 Who does Kenny love?
  2 Who loves Kenny?

c 1 What kind of people does Kenny dislike?
  2 What kind of people (probably) dislike Kenny?

23 Copy and complete the chart with examples from Activity 22.

Asking about the object: *Who/What* with do/does	Asking about the subject: *Who/What* without do or does
Who do you admire? (I admire) Nicole Kidman. What programmes do you watch? (I watch) comedies and soap operas.	Who admires Nicole Kidman? I do. What makes you laugh? Comedies (do).

→ see 12C in the Mini-grammar

24 Look at Kenny. Answer the questions in Activity 22. Then answer the questions about yourself. (Who do you admire? Who admires you? etc.)

25 Read the sentences.

Ask questions about the sections underlined using the given question word.

Write the answers using the underlined words. The first one is done for you.

a <u>Everybody</u> wants to be a millionaire. Who?

Q   Who wants to be a millionaire?
A   Everybody does.

b Everybody wants to be <u>a millionaire</u>. What?
c Many people read <u>magazines about celebrities</u>. What?
d <u>Many people</u> read magazines about celebrities. Who?
e <u>Celebrities</u> don't like photographers. Who?
f Celebrities don't like <u>photographers</u>. What?
g Monkeys eat <u>nuts and fruit</u>. What?
h <u>Monkeys</u> eat nuts and fruit. Who?

26 Complete the questions with verbs from the box.
Who does these things in your family?
Answer the questions.

a Who watches a lot of television? My brother does.
b Who .... talking about pop music?
c Who .... a sporting star?
d Who .... soap operas?
e Who .... on the phone a lot?
f Who .... fashion magazines?
g Who .... a lot of friends?
h Who .... English very well?

watch
admire
buy
enjoy
like
have
do
speak (x2)

27 In pairs Ask your partner the questions in Activity 26.
Then ask an extra question.

Example: STUDENT A: Who watches a lot of television?

STUDENT B: My brother does.

STUDENT A: What programme does he watch most?

STUDENT B: His favourite programme is The Simpsons.

Study functions: discussing opinions

28 Look at the picture. Can you guess what the people are talking about?

NEXT on 5 Soap Time
The Rich Cry Too

Now listen to Track 15. Were you right?

29 Who says these things, Jane or Lisa?

   a What do you think of soaps now?
   b I hate soaps. They're silly stories.
   c No they're not. Oh, Shhhhh. It's about to start.
   d Well, I don't agree. I think they're really exciting.
   e What, now? I can't. *The Rich Cry Too* is about to begin. Don't you watch it?
   f You're joking! Soap operas are for people who have nothing better to do.
   g Actually, this is exciting!
   h Do you want to go out for pizza?

30 In pairs Put the lines in Activity 29 in the correct order to rewrite the dialogue. Then read it to another pair. Are your dialogues the same? Listen to Track 15 again to check your dialogues.

31 Copy and complete the chart with phrases in blue from Activity 29.

> Asking for an opinion:
>
> Giving an opinion:
> Agreeing:
> You're right.
> I agree.
> Questioning opinions:
> Do you really think so?
> Disagreeing:

Can you add any more words or phrases to your chart?

32 Listen to Track 16. Copy and complete the lists with the words you hear.

Words which mean 'really good': great, terrific
Words which mean 'really bad': terrible

33 Exchange opinions about the things in the pictures. Use the phrases in the chart and the words in Activity 32. Listen to Track 16 again, if you need to.

Example: STUDENT A: What do you think of ......?
              STUDENT B: I think it's ....
              STUDENT A: Do you? I think ....

34 In groups Make a list of popular TV programmes, music, films and magazines that everyone knows.

One student says one of the items on the list. The others give and exchange opinions about the item.

Speaking: deciding what to watch

35 In groups of five You and four friends want to watch different programmes on television. The DVD recorder and the video machine are broken!

STUDENT A: go to **Activity 3 in the Activity Bank on page 134.**

STUDENT B: go to **Activity 5 in the Activity Bank on page 135.**

STUDENT C: go to **Activity 8 in the Activity Bank on page 136.**

STUDENT D: go to **Activity 25 in the Activity Bank on page 140.**

STUDENT E: go to **Activity 28 in the Activity Bank on page 141.**

a When is your programme? Read the TV guide.
b Together, find a solution to the problem. Can you be fair to everyone?

Channel 1
6.00 *News and Views*
7.00 *Crime Report*
7.30 *World Cup Final. Kick off at 8.00*
9.00 *News and Views*

Channel 2
6.30 *Round the Corner – game show*
7.30 *Japan Today – documentary*
8.15 *Animal Hospital – reality*

Channel 3
6.00 *The Great Pop Concert – live from Hyde Park*
8.00 *Film*
         The Empire Strikes Back

Channel 4
6.45 *The Greens – golf highlights*
7.30 *Politics Today*

Channel 5
6.00 *Home and Away.*
6.30 *Family Affairs*
7.30 *Along the Meridian – travel documentary*

36 Compare your solution with other groups. Who has the best solution?

Pronunciation: /ʒ/ and /ʃ/

37 Listen to Track 17. Number the words in the correct order, 1- 8.

| television | usual | information | fashion |
| decision | obsession | solution | conclusion |

38 Listen to Track 17 again. Do the words have the sound /ʒ/ like television or /ʃ/ like information? Copy the chart, write the words under the correct sound.

Words with the sound /ʒ/

Words with the sound /ʃ/

39 Listen to Track 18 and repeat the words.
a television
b conclusion
c usual
d decision
e information
f solution
g obsession
h fashion

Can you think of any more words with the same sounds? Add them to the chart.

UNIT 4
Making a living

Reading: crocodile hunter

Just learning: *guessing word meaning in a reading text*

When you find a new word or phrase in a text, you can try to guess its meaning. Ask:

a What is the word; a noun, verb, adjective etc?

b Is the word explained in the text? (Read to the end to see.)

c Does it look like other words you know in English?

d Does it look like a word in your language? This will often help you understand.

---

1 Look at the pictures. Read the title. Make a list of words you would use to describe the occupation and the people who do it.

Example: dangerous, stupid, brave

Compare your list with your partner. Do you agree?

2 **Quick reading** Find out:

a the name of the crocodile hunter
b his wife's name and her occupation
c where their Reptile and Fauna Park is
d what other animals the couple catch

The crocodile hunter

When he was six Steve Irwin got his first pet animal. It was a very large snake. This was the start of his hobby and by the age of 12 he was helping his father catch crocodiles, or 'jump crocs' as he calls it.

When someone with a pet snake at six years old grows up, what does he do? He becomes a reptile expert, a herpetologist, or 'herp' for short. And Steve Irwin became Australia's most famous crocodile hunter. Now Steve and his wife Terri, an American lion tamer, run a wildlife park in Queensland, Australia.

Although Steve is called a 'crocodile hunter' he doesn't kill the animals; instead, he moves 'problem' crocodiles to safe environments. These rogue crocodiles live in popular fishing and swimming areas where tourists like to go and so, of course, they are a danger to people. Steve can move crocs up to 8 feet long (2.44 metres) with his bare hands.

But the Irwins don't just catch crocodiles. They also catch dangerous snakes and 'milk', or collect, their venom to make anti-toxin (that's medicine to help people with snake bites). And how does Steve catch snakes? With his bare hands of course!

The Irwins first became famous through their popular television series, the Crocodile Hunter. 'Saltwater crocodiles are the largest reptiles in the world,' says Steve. 'People are scared of them and shoot them. Through our programme, people can learn about these animals and learn to respect them.'

So, are you interested in reptiles? Are you looking for an exciting, unusual occupation? Then maybe you too can become a herpetologist, like Steve. But please don't try his tricks at home!

3 Vocabulary Find these words and phrases in the text. Guess their meaning. Make a note of how you made your guesses.

a 'jump crocs'
b 'milk' (a snake's venom)
c herpetologist
d anti-toxin
e rogue crocodiles
f venom
g with his bare hands
h saltwater crocodiles

Example: jump crocs – to
catch crocodiles: explained
in text

4 Find three more new words or phrases in the article. Ask your partner to try and explain their meaning.

5 Take a closer look

What …
a is a herpetologist?
b does Steve Irwin do with the crocs he catches?
c was Terri's previous occupation?

Why …
d did Steve become a crocodile hunter?
e does he catch snakes?
f does Steve think their programme is important?
g do people shoot crocodiles?

Study grammar: present continuous and present simple

6 Read the pairs of sentences. Are the meanings the same or different?

a Steve usually works with crocodiles.
  Steve is working with saltwater crocodiles.
b Terri makes documentaries.
  Terri is making a new documentary.
c The Irwins work in Queensland.
  The Irwins are working in a different part of Australia for a few weeks.

7 Read the explanations. Then complete the sentences a – f.

We use the present simple to talk about things that happen regularly or habitually.	We use the present continuous to talk about things happening at the time you are speaking or to talk about things that are temporary.
I help my father at the shop. *I (normally) work on Saturdays.*	*I am helping my father at the shop (at the moment = it's 10.30 now).* *I am working on Sundays this month.*

→ see 10A and 10B in the Mini-grammar

a Listen! What song .... (play) on the radio?
b I think it's Dido. They .... (play) this song all the time.
c What .... that man .... (do) in your garden?
d Oh him! He .... (cut) the trees. Watch out! Don't go near.
e .... you .... (live) here permanently?
f No. I .... (stay) here for three months. I'm doing a course at a college near here.

a bouncer   b dog walker   c pest controller

d roadie   e personal trainer

f Disc jockey (DJ)

8 In pairs Look at the pictures. Talk about what the people are doing.

Example:

STUDENT A: In picture a, the boy is probably asking for directions.

STUDENT B: I'm not sure what the pest controller is doing. Is he fighting?

9 Who does what? Match the activities with the occupations in Activity 8. The first one is done for you.

This person…

a stands at the door of clubs *bouncer*

b looks after other people's dogs

c organises exercise programmes

d plays pop music on the radio

e throws out people who behave badly

f moves equipment for musicians

g catches and kills pests, like rats

h plays records at clubs and parties

i helps other people get fit

j takes dogs for a walk

k gets rid of insects, like cockroaches

l helps prepare equipment for pop concerts

10 Write sentences about what the people in Activity 8 do and what they are doing in the pictures.

Example: *Bouncers stand at the door of clubs and throw out people who behave badly. In the picture, the bouncer is probably checking a boy's ID card.*

Now go to Activity 4 in the Activity Bank on page 135. Were you right?

Study vocabulary: jobs and work

11 Look at the dictionary entries. Then complete the sentences with *job* or *work*.

> **Job n.** [C] **1** an activity you do to earn your living, especially if you are working for somebody else. *I have a job in a shop.* **2** a specific piece of work that has to be done. *Who does all the jobs around the house?*
>
> **Work n.** [U] **1** an activity you are paid for doing, especially regularly. *What work do you do?* **2** a general word when you are talking about several different jobs. *He's got a lot of work to do.*

a .... is a noun that has a plural.

b I have a lot of .... to do at the office.

c Nat's .... is to wash cars.

d A roadie's .... sounds fun.

e I have several boring .... to do today, like cleaning my room.

f Mara is looking for a .... for the holidays.

g Are you looking for .... ? Look at the small ads in the paper.

12 Match the *work + preposition* phrases in the left-hand column with the phrases in the right-hand column.

a work in	1 a fast food restaurant
b work as	2 small children
c work for	3 a project
d work on	4 a computer programmer
e work out	5 a large company
f work with	6 the solution of a problem

13 Choose phrases from Activity 12 to complete the sentences.

a Joe likes helping people. He .... problem teenagers.

b I have to .... my presentation for tomorrow's class. It's still not very good.

c Do you still .... the same company?

d The teacher can't give us any help. We have to .... the answer for ourselves.

e Julie wants to .... a model.

f I hate .... this place!

14 Make notes about yourself. Give reasons.

Who/what would you like to work for?
Who would you like to work with?
What are you working on now?
Where do other people in your family work?
What would you like to work as?
What problem in English can't you work out?

15 Compare your answers with your partner.

Example: STUDENT A: *Who would you like to work for?*

STUDENT B: *I want to work for a television channel.*

STUDENT A: *Why?*

STUDENT B: *I think it is interesting.*

16 In pairs Answer these questions.

a Are quiz shows popular in your country?
b Which are the most popular?
c What do contestants have to do?
d Look at the picture. Do you know the game they are playing?
e What do you think the panel have to do?

17 Listen to Track 19 to check your answer to the last question in Activity 16.

18 Listen to Track 19 again. Write short answers to the panel's questions.

a Do you work with animals?
b Is your occupation dangerous?
c Do you work in a special place?
d Do you enjoy your job?

Can you guess Jason's job? Listen to Track 20 to check your answer.

19 Listen to Track 20 again. What words do you hear in these blanks?

PANELLIST A: Sorry. OK. Do you kill the
(a) .... you work with?
JASON: Yes! Yes I have to (b) .... them!
PANELLIST B: Right, I think we've got it! Are you
a ... Are you one of those (c) .... who kill
rats, or bad insects or (d) .... like that? Do
you kill pests like that? Are you a – what is it?
PANELLIST C: (e) .... controller?
PANELLIST A: Yes, that's it! A pest (f)............? Are
you a (g) ....?
JASON: (h) ....! I am a pest controller.

20 Write a list of the rules for playing *What's my Job*?
Listen to Tracks 19 & 20 again if you want.

Study pronunciation: intonation of *yes/no* questions

21 Listen to Track 21. Does the speaker's voice go up, or down?

a Do you like your job?

b Do you enjoy it?

c Is it dangerous?

d Do you have a good job?

e Is the money good?

22 Listen to Track 22 and repeat the questions you hear.

23 In pairs Write five *yes/no* questions by yourself. Swap your questions with your partner. Can he/she read them correctly? Can you read your partner's questions correctly?

Example: *Are you happy?*

Speaking: What's my Job?

24 In groups You are going to play 'What's my Job?'.

a Panel: You want to guess the guest's job. Think of 20 good questions to ask.
Guest: Choose an occupation. Make notes about the things you do.

b Play 'What's my Job?' Use the rules from Activity 20.
The panel guess the job in 20 questions: they win!
The panel can't guess the job in 20 questions: the Guest wins!

c The 'Guests' move to different groups. How many times can you win?

Study grammar: present continuous with future meaning

25 Listen to Track 23. Put the pictures in the right order.

26 You can use the present continuous to talk about the present [P], and to talk about the future [F]. Are the underlined verbs about the future or the present?

a We're playing in the final on Sunday, so we're training hard.

b I'm meeting my client tomorrow, so I'm checking the plans.

c I'm practising because I'm taking my driving test tomorrow.

d I'm working hard now, but on Saturday we're having a party!

Which meaning usually takes a time expression, present or future?

→ see 4B in the Mini-grammar

27 Copy and complete the chart with the time expressions in the list. You can use some of them with both future and present meaning.

> now   tomorrow   today   at 8 o'clock   next week
> on 25th May   on Tuesday   at this moment   this week
> in the summer   Monday afternoon

Time expressions for the present	Time expressions for the future
now	tomorrow

Can you add more time expressions to the chart?

28 Copy the page of the diary. Write in your firm plans for the week.

Week 12

Monday	Thursday
a.m.	a.m.
p.m.	p.m.
Tuesday	Friday
a.m.	a.m.
p.m.	p.m.
Wednesday	Saturday
a.m.	
	Sunday
p.m.	

29 In pairs Do not show your diary to your partner!

Look at your diaries and find a time when you can do something together.

Example: STUDENT A: *What are you doing on Wednesday afternoon?*

STUDENT B: *I'm taking a piano lesson.*

Study functions: likes and dislikes

30 Listen to Track 24. Which advertisements are the people looking at?

Situations vacant

Wanted A baby sitter for 3 lovely children ages 6, 4 and 2. Evenings.
Call 02028657213

Making Waves are looking for junior staff. This could be the beginning in a career in hairdressing. Call Jess on 082749

Calling animal lovers The Animal Shelter is looking for people to help with unloved animals. Interested? Phone 04978826

Cool Gear are looking for cool guys to work at our new branch. Good basic salary. Discount on all our clothes. Phone the manager on 095739 or 095720

Burger Lads are hiring now for the holiday period. Good pay. Come and see us! 297 Main Street

Maths tutor required. Are you good at Maths? Are you patient? Then you are the person we are looking for. Call Mrs Rock on 020 8595637

31 Listen to Track 24 again. Who says these things, Fred or Bella?

a Nah, there is nothing I fancy.

b I like children.

c I don't mind children.

d That's not for me.

e I'm not keen on animals.

f I love animals.

g I can't stand fast food places.

h It's not that bad.

32 Copy and complete the chart with the phrases in Activity 31.

Ways to say you like something
I fancy …

Ways to say you don't like something (or it's not right for you)
I don't fancy … There's nothing I fancy.

33 Copy the *like-dislike* line below. Using the phrases from Activity 32 and the words in the box, say where the words and phrases fit on your *like-dislike* line.

dislike   hate   like   love   not like

extreme dislike | ————————————— | like very very much

34 In pairs You are looking for a temporary job. Read the 'small ads' in Activity 30 on page 35 and complete the tasks which follow. You can listen to Track 24 again if you want.

a Student A, suggest jobs to your partner. Give reasons.

b Student B, listen to your partner's suggestions. Say what you like/don't like about the jobs. Use expressions from Activities 32 and 33.

Example: STUDENT A: How about a job in
.... It sounds good.

STUDENT B: That's not for me. I think it's boring.

Writing: small ads

35 Read the ads. Who is offering a job? Who is looking for a job?

36 Put the following information in the same sequence as in the advertisements on the right.

Ad A

a the name of the person looking for a job
b the person's skills
c a contact number
d extra, important information about the person
e what the person is looking for

Ad B

a the name of the company
b what the company is looking for
c what the company offers
d what the company needs
e a contact number

37 Complete the following tasks:

a You are looking for staff. Write a small ad for a particular job. Include the things on the list in Activity 36 and write them in the same order.

b You are looking for work. Write a small ad. Include the things on the list in Activity 36 and write them in the same order.

38 Swap your ads with other people. Choose a job that sounds good for you. How many people are interested in the job you are offering?

A **Wanted**

I am a student looking for temporary office work.
I can speak English and I have good computer skills.
I have no experience but
I am a fast learner.

Please ring Carrie on 3759670, evenings.

B **WANTED**

We are looking for temporary staff in our offices. We require:
Good presentation
Good English
Good computing skills
We offer:
A good salary
Free sports club
Free lunches at the company's restaurant
Call 75953795 NOW!
Kimber and Kimber Associates

On the move

Reading: the station

1 **Quick reading** What kind of story does the extract come from?

   a a romance/love story
   b a science fiction story
   c a thriller/spy story
   d a horror story

Talk to other students. Do they agree with you?

2 **Take a closer look** Look at the picture and read the text again. There are four mistakes in it. What are they?

When he came into the station, Ferdy looked down at all the people below him. Ah yes. There she was. Amelie. The beautiful Amelie, with her long black hair and her incredible blue blue eyes. She was waiting for him.

Ferdy's eyes scanned the scene in front of him, and then he looked up. Above him two men were working on the roof. He could see them through the glass. What were they doing there? Perhaps they were cleaning the glass. But perhaps they weren't.

He tried to act normally. He got onto the escalator and went down towards the platforms just like any other normal person. But that was the problem. He wasn't normal. He was different from other people.

Opposite him was the entrance to the Platform – her platform. Amelie was standing under the number 7. Perhaps everything was OK.

But then he saw two young women in yellow hard hats. They were standing by the coffee stall. He noticed something. They weren't talking or drinking coffee. They were watching everyone in the station, but when he looked at them, they looked away.

Suddenly he heard a noise. Someone inside the ticket office was shouting into a mobile phone. He turned his head. It was an old man, and next to him was a woman. His wife?

Nothing to worry about. But then the old man saw him. He stopped shouting. He took his mobile phone from his ear. He just stared.

Platform 7 was in front of him now. Amelie saw him. She smiled.

Suddenly a woman walked between him and Amelie. She didn't look happy. Then he knew. He was in danger.

Ferdy looked behind him. There was no one. He turned round and ran back up the escalator and into the street. He heard Amelie call his name.

There were three men standing outside and they were waiting for him.

3 Vocabulary Look at the words in blue in the text. Choose the ones you know and explain the meanings to your partner.

Now match the words with these definitions.

a looked from side to side very quickly to get a general view
b moving stairs
c the top part of the building
d the same as other people – not different
e be unhappy/anxious about something and think about it a lot
f looked at someone for a long time – without moving your head
g turned quickly and looked at something different
h very, very beautiful, fantastic

4 In groups Read the descriptions. Which one is the best?

He (Ferdy) wasn't normal. He was different from other people.

a Ferdy is a bank robber. Amelie is his girlfriend. All the other people are police.
b Ferdy is a spy working for a foreign government. Amelie wants to give him secrets.
c Ferdy is a good man, but some people think he did something bad. Amelie is his only friend. She wants to help him.

Ferdy and Amelie do meet two days later. Invent the conversation they have.

Study grammar: prepositions of place

5 Choose a word or phrase from the box to complete each sentence. Use each word or phrase once only.

above behind below between in in front of inside
on top of next to opposite outside under

a The Just Films building is .... a church and a supermarket.
b The Just Films building is .... Dover Street.
c The Just Films building is .... the supermarket.
d The Just Films building is .... the station.
e The car park is .... the Just Films building.
f The film star is .... the Just Films building.
g The third floor of the Just Films building is .... the second floor and .... the fifth floor.
h There are a lot of photographers .... the entrance.
i There is a limousine .... the Just Films building.
j There's a helicopter .... the Just Films building.
k There's a tunnel .... Dover Street.

→ see 9A in the Mini-grammar

6 Student A, look at the picture above.

Student B, go to Activity 6 in the Activity Bank on page 135.

Ask each other questions to find as many differences between your two pictures as possible.

Example: Is the limousine in front of the Just Films building?

7 Look at words and phrases that are used with *at*, *in* or both (when talking about place). Complete the tasks which follow.

at ...	in ...	at ... or in ...
... the bus stop	... Turkey	... the cinema
... the entrance to	... the living room	... Steve's house
the station	... the office	... (the) hospital
... home		... the station
... work		... a café

a Look at the pictures. Decide where you think the people are.

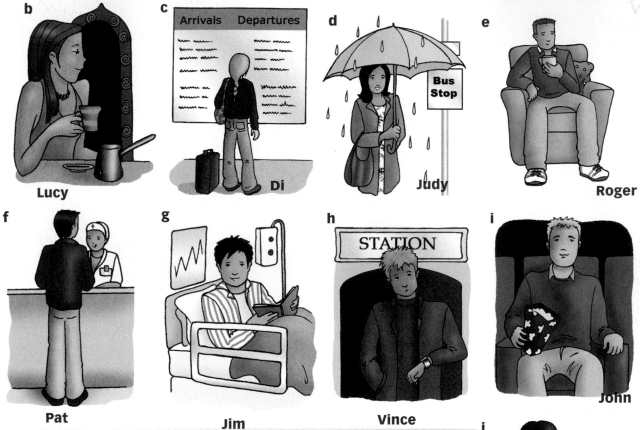

Steve / Jack

Lucy

Di

Judy

Roger

Pat

Jim

Vince

John

Hazel

b Compare your answers with your partner.

Example: STUDENT A: I think Jack's at home

STUDENT B: I'm not sure. I think he's at Steve's house.

8 Tell your partner where friends and members of your family are at the moment. Say where the place is.

Example: My sister's at work at her school. It's in Green Street, opposite the new cinema.

Study vocabulary: public transport

9 Match the places in the box with the pictures.

> (railway/underground) station   airport
> bus (coach) station   ferry terminal

A

B

10 In groups Copy the chart below. Complete it with as many of the words from the box as possible for the pictures A – D. Some of the words can go in more than one column.

Airport	Coach Station	Ferry Terminal	Station
Check-in desk			

> bay   barrier   check-in desk   train   escalator
> gate   lift   passport control   plane   platform
> ticket machine   ticket office   train

C

D

11 Complete the announcements with the verbs in the box. Use some of them more than once.

> arrive   board   change   check in
> go   leave   take

a Passengers can .... the plane at gate 34.

b .... the 36B bus to the city centre.

c .... the ferry 30 minutes before departure.

d .... to terminal 2 for flights to Asia.

e The flight .... at three thirty.

f .... the lift to the second floor.

g The train .... from platform 5.

h .... to gate 36.

i The train from Washington .... at five minutes past three.

j .... trains at Birmingham Central.

k You will have to .... planes at Dallas airport.

l .... 2 hours before your plane leaves.

12 Using as many words and phrases as possible from Activities 9 – 11:

a Describe a journey you do at least twice a week.

b Describe how you can get to a different part of your city, town or country by public transport.

Study functions: arranging to meet

13 Complete the dialogue with one word for each blank.

KIM: What time shall we meet, Max?
MAX: I could be (1) .... by about 11.
KIM: OK, (2) .... do you suggest?
MAX: Well, Kim, I could (3) .... at the top of the escalator, you know, (4) .... the entrance.
KIM: I've got a better idea. How (5) .... under the clock by platform 3?
MAX: OK. That sounds (6) .... Eleven o'clock it is then. (7) .... the clock.
KIM: Fine. See you (8) ....

Listen to Track 25. Did you have the same words as Kim and Max?

14 Copy and complete the chart with phrases a – l.

Asking for suggestions	What time shall we meet?
Making suggestions	I could meet you at the top of the escalator.
Offering alternatives	I've got a better idea.
Agreeing	Fine. See you at 11.

a Sounds great!
b Have you got any ideas/suggestions?
c How about the café on Logan Street?
d Let's meet under the clock.
e Let's say eight thirty.
f OK, eight o'clock it is, then.
g Or we could meet at the bus stop.
h That sounds good.
i We could meet at eight o'clock.
j What's the best time to meet?
k Where do you suggest?
l Why don't we go to the Twenty-two club?

15 Change the words in blue in Activity 14 to make new questions and statements.

Example: *Where shall we meet?*

16 Make conversations in which you arrange to meet for:

a a sporting event
b a film
c a concert
d a meal

Listening: team building

17 Look at the picture on page 43. Choose the best answer, a, b or c.

a The people are from an office in the city. It is Saturday. They are all in the country for two days – for an 'Activity Weekend'. Some of them don't really want to do the activity, but they all do it.

b The people are from an office in the city. It is Saturday. They are all in the country for two days – for an 'Activity Weekend'. Some of them don't really want to do the activity and one person doesn't do it.

c The people are from an office in the city. It is Saturday. They are all in the country for two days – for an 'Activity Weekend'. Everyone wants to do the activity but one person doesn't do it.

Listen to Track 26. Were you right?

18 Listen to Track 26 again. Put the pictures in the right order.

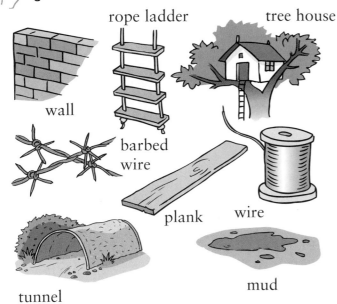

rope ladder

tree house

wall

barbed wire

plank

wire

tunnel

mud

19 Choose the correct verbs. Listen to Track 26 to help you if, necessary.

| climb crawl drop hang jump |
| make run walk |

a .... towards the wall.
b .... up the wall.
c .... down the other side.
d .... through the tunnel.
e .... the rope ladder.
f .... along the wooden plank.
g .... from the wire.
h .... your way along the wire.
i .... into the mud.
j .... under the barbed wire.
k .... back to me.

20 Dictate-a-course Make your own activity course. Follow these instructions:

a Draw the parts of the course (wall, wire, etc) in a sequence you like.

b Write sentences to explain the course. You can use the sentence ideas in this box and the phrases from Activity 19.

First you ....

After you .... , you ....

When you get there/to the............... , you ....

c Dictate your course to a partner. Your partner draws the course.

Pronunciation: three vowel sounds

21 Listen to Track 27. Copy and complete the chart with the words in the box. Look at the underlined sound in two- or three-syllable words.

A̲melie back clock drop front hang jump la̲dder mud o̲pposite plank pla̲tform scanned so̲me̲one son top tu̲nnel u̲nder

/ɒ/ - cop	/æ/ - cap	/ʌ/ - cup

22 Play Track 27 again. Say the words after the speakers

Speaking: press conference

23 In groups Look at the three pictures and complete the tasks which follow.

a

b

c

a Decide on names for the people in the pictures.

b Think of questions for each character (ask about their jobs, what they like, what a normal day is like for them, why they do their job, how they prefer to travel, etc).

24 A student sits at the front of the class. The student is one of the celebrities in the pictures.

The class are all journalists. They interview the celebrity.

Study grammar: prepositions of movement

25 Read the description of the first minutes of a new film 'The Driver'. Put the pictures in order.

THE DRIVER

In the first scene Sally drives onto a ferry. In the second scene she is driving off the ferry at Jebel Ali. She drives towards the airport, and then through the new airport tunnel to Terminal 1. She goes into the terminal building and meets her friend.

Then we see her driving over the Ras Al Khaimah bridge. She drives along the coast road with her friend. Suddenly she turns into the desert. She drives up a sand dune and down the other side. There are two men and three camels waiting for them... .

26 In pairs Check your understanding by describing the pictures.

Example: STUDENT A: She's driving up a sand dune.

STUDENT B: Picture j?

→ see 9B in the Mini-grammar

27 Look at the picture and find the treasure. What's the best way to get to it? Plan your route and then compare your route with a partner.

Start

How similar is your route to the rest of the class?

Writing: direction emails

28 Read the email and choose the correct map.

In

Delete　Reply　Reply All　Forward　Compose　Mailboxes　Get Mail　Junk

Tom

Great to hear you're coming to the party.

When you get to the station, turn right and go along Station Road for about five minutes. Take the third left and go along that street. Take the second right and we are on the right, opposite the park.

See you tomorrow.

Sal

29 Write directions for the other two maps in Activity 28. Use language from the email (look at the language in the box).

30 Write emails to your English-speaking friends explaining how to get to your house from the station, metro station, or bus stop.

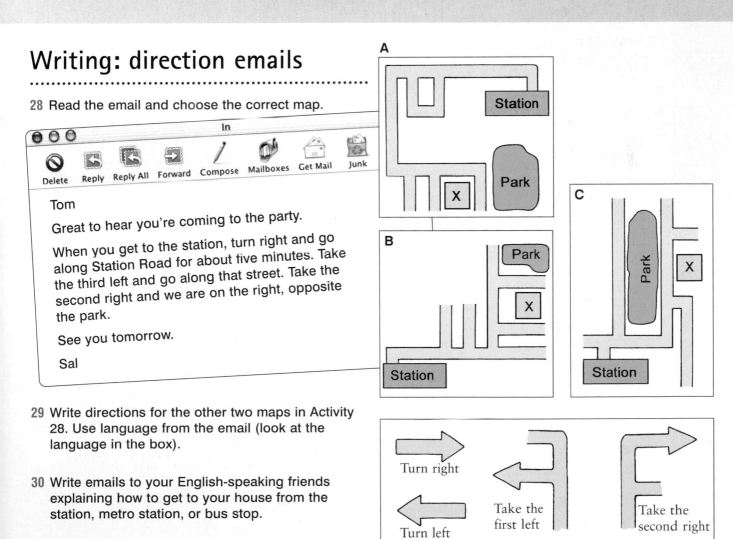

A

Station

Park

X

B

Park

X

Station

C

Park

X

Station

Turn right

Turn left

Take the first left

Take the second right

Reading: short-term and long-term memory

1 **Discuss the following questions:**

  a Why do we forget people's names and faces?
  b What is long-term memory? What is short-term memory?
  c We forget faces but we remember how to ride a bicycle. What's the difference?

Quick reading Does the text say the same things as you?

I want to know about... MEMORY

Dr Gita Patel, a memory expert, answers your questions.

Q: I met a guy at a party. We met again a few days later and I couldn't remember his name! I felt bad. What's wrong with my memory?

A: We all forget things. We throw away information that we don't need any more. You put the man's name in your *short-term memory.* That's the bit of your brain that keeps things you don't need to remember for very long – like a telephone number you only use once. You forgot the man's name because it wasn't very important to you.

Q: What is long-term memory?

A: *Long-term memory* is where we keep information we need to remember for a long time. It is like a filing cabinet with different drawers. One drawer contains memories of things that happened to you a long time ago, like your first day at school or a summer holiday. This is your *episodic* memory. It stores the episodes that make up your life. You don't think about these things all the time. But then something, like a smell or a song brings that memory back and suddenly you remember everything about it. Another drawer is your *semantic* memory. In this drawer the brain keeps information like important historical dates and facts about your country. Your brain only opens this drawer when you need to use the information, for example in a test.

Q: People say you never forget how to do things like riding a bicycle. Is this true?

A: Yes. This is called *procedural* memory because it stores procedures, or the way to do things. It helps you to remember skills you learned in your life, things like how to ride a bike or how to use a mobile phone. These memories stay in the brain all your life.

2 Take a closer look True (T) or False (F)?

a Everybody forgets things.
b We forget information that we don't need anymore.
c The writer of the first question really wanted to remember the name of the man she met.
d Dates (e.g. from history) are stored in the same place as events in your life.
e Semantic memory can be useful in exams.
f A smell can bring back memories.
g Procedural memory allows you to remember telephone numbers.

3 Copy and complete the chart with one or two notes to help you remember the meanings.

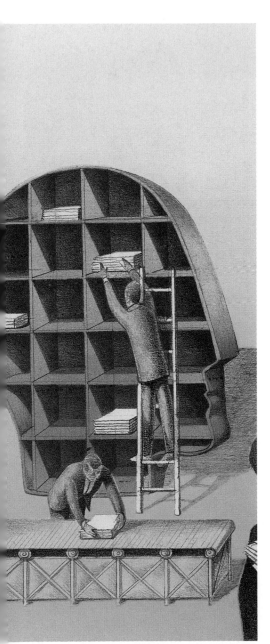

	NOTES
Short-term memory	
Long-term memory	
Episodic memory	
Procedural memory	
Semantic memory	

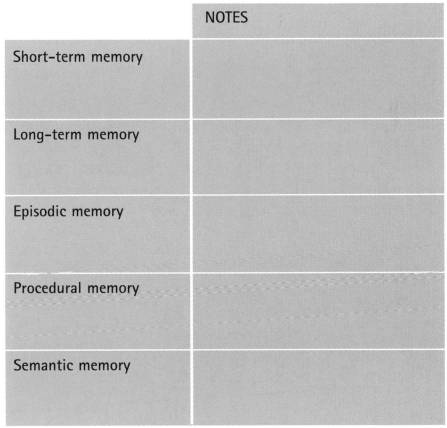

Compare your chart with your partner.

4 Vocabulary Find the words in blue which mean:

a A piece of furniture to keep files in. (noun)
b Not right. (adjective)
c A particular event in your life. (noun)
d The ability to remember things in the past. (noun)
e Particular events or experiences you remember from the past. (noun)
f To put or keep in a special place. (verb)
g To bring back a memory. (verb)

Study grammar: the past simple

5   Copy the following verb lists. Write the base form of the verbs. The first two are done for you.

Regular verbs	Irregular verbs		
laughed laugh	forgot	forget	met
memorised	found		put
repeated	felt		tried
wanted	gave		wrote
	had		

Add two useful regular verbs and two useful irregular verbs to the lists. You can look at page 44 in the Mini-booklet to help you with irregular verbs.

6   Choose a verb from the box in Activity 5 for each blank, a – k. Put it in the right form.

> I (a) ......*met*..... an old friend in the street. She (b) .... me her phone number. I didn't (c) .... it down but I (d) .... it and (e) .... it many times in my head. The next day I (f) .... to phone my friend but I couldn't remember the number. Luckily I (g) .... her in the phone book. She laughed. 'Of course you (h) .... the number. Why didn't you write it down? At school you always (i)................... a terrible memory,' she said. I (j) .... silly. Did I really have a terrible memory then? Well, not anymore! Now, where did I (k) .... my keys?

7   Read the text in Activity 6 again. Find and copy:

   a   a negative sentence in the past
   b   two 'wh' questions in the past
   c   a question in the past that you can answer 'yes' or 'no'.

   → see 8A in the Mini-grammar

8   Choose the correct form of the verbs in brackets and complete the sets of questions.

   a   What is your earliest memory of school? What .... that day? (happen) Who .... you .... ? (meet) What .... the names of your first friends? (be) Who .... your favourite teacher? (be)

   b   Can you ride a bicycle, use a tin opener, or use a mobile phone? How long ago .... you .... those things? (learn)

   c   Pick an important event in the history of your country. When exactly .... the event .... ? (happen) What .... the people .... ? (do)

   d   When .... you last .... the phone to call someone who is not a friend? (use) Why .... you .... ? (phone) What .... the phone number? (be)

9   How good is your memory? Answer the questions in Activity 8. Then ask your partner the same questions.

Study vocabulary: life stages

1974 1980 1990 1996 1996 2001 2004

10 Choose words from the box to go with the pictures. Sometimes more than one word is possible.

> adolescence (teens)   adulthood   birth   childhood
> education   marriage   parenthood   romance   work

11 **In pairs** Copy and complete the chart with the verbs in the box. Use a dictionary if necessary.

> to graduate from   to fall in love   to die   to have a baby
> to get married   to start school   to marry someone
> to work as a...   to be keen on someone   to be dead
> to get a job   to be born

12 Fill in the blanks with the past simple of the verbs in Activity 11.

birth	education	work	romance	marriage	death
to be born					

a Mark was born in 1974. On 29th January, Mr and Mrs Thomas .... a baby. They called him Mark, after his father.

b Little Mark .... school when he was 6 years old.

c When he was 16, Mark went out with Susan. He .... on her but their romance did not last long and after school, he didn't see her again.

d Mark .... university in 1996 and soon .... a job in a computer company, where he .... a programmer.

e At work, Mark met Susan again. This time they .... for real.

f Mark .... his childhood sweetheart in 2001. They .... on a balloon! It was a fantastic wedding and everyone had fun.

g Mark's dad is now .... He .... a few years ago. Now Susan is expecting a baby. If it's a boy, she wants to call him Mark, after his dad and granddad.

13 Make notes about the life of a member of your family. Use the verbs in Activity 11.

Example: *dad – born 1950*

14 **In pairs** Tell your partner about a member of your family. How many things do your stories have in common?

Example:

STUDENT A: *My dad was born in the 50s.*

STUDENT B: *My parents were born in the 50s, too.*

Listening: the soundtrack of our lives

15 Copy and complete the chart with names of popular songs in your country. You have two minutes.

Romantic songs
Songs for dancing
Songs for children
Traditional songs

16 In pairs Who is the music expert? Complete the tasks that follow.

  a Compare your charts. Who wrote down the most songs?
  b Sing or hum the songs on each other's charts. How many can you sing or hum?

  Who is the music expert?

17 Listen to Track 28. Who says these things, Sophie, Mandy or Mandy's boyfriend Bill? Sophie speaks first.

  a 'I didn't know you liked romantic songs.'
  b 'Songs are like the soundtrack of our lives.'
  c 'Every time I hear the song I can remember that summer as if it was yesterday.'
  d 'You sound like old people talking about old times!'
  e 'I bet you have a song that brings back memories.'
  f 'You can't remember the song they were playing when we met?'
  g 'I can remember the tune but I can't think of the name.'

18 Listen to Track 28 again. Who

  a liked a boy called Jerry at school?
  b doesn't usually like romantic songs?
  c used to sing in a band?
  d hears a song and then remembers summer as if it was yesterday?
  e thinks her friends are like married people?
  f has a bad memory?
  g thinks their friends are like old people?
  h is a little cross?

19 Write a list of special songs that bring back memories of things in your life. Tell your partner about the songs and what they remind you of.

Example: One of my favourite songs is 'Imagine' by John Lennon. My mother sang it all the time when I was a child.

> **Just learning:** *using everything you know for listening*
>
> When you listen to English on the radio, on the Internet or on a CD or tape, use everything you know! What kind of listening is it (an advertisement, a conversation, a news broadcast, etc)? What do you know about advertisements, conversations, etc? What do you expect?
>
> Next, listen to the other sounds. Are the speakers outside or inside? In a street or a café?
>
> Finally, listen to the speakers' 'feelings'. Do they sound happy or sad, angry or pleased?
>
> All of these things help us to understand the words.

Study pronunciation: intonation (exclamations)

20 Listen to these exclamations on Track 29. Are the speakers interested and/or amused or bored and/or disapproving?

a How funny!
b How stupid!
c How silly!
d How boring!
e How lovely!

21 Repeat the exclamations with the correct intonation.

22 Listen to Track 30 and react to what people say. Use the exclamations in Activity 20.

Study grammar: *used to*

23 Read the quotes. How old is Mrs Hall – around 60, around 80 or around 100?

24 Read the quotes in Activity 23. Copy and complete the chart.

We didn't use to have a car. They were very new and very expensive!

We didn't have a phone. There used to be just one in our village – for emergencies.

When I was a child we used to play board games. There was no TV!

Girls didn't use to stay in school for very long. I left school when I was 12.

We used to watch a movie occasionally. Movies were silent then.

Talking about past habits: used to
Affirmative:
Negative:
Questions: Did you use to listen to records? What did you use to do for fun?

Check your answers with Activity 9 in the Activity Bank on page 136. Were you right?

→ see 8C in the Mini-grammar

25 Choose the correct form of *used to* with the words in brackets to complete the sentences.

  a The Halls (have) .... a family holiday at the beach every summer. Then the children grew up and everything changed.

  b They (not go out often) .... But they had lots of fun. The whole family (play board games) .... together. Television changed all that.

  c Mrs Hall loved the fashion in the 1950s. Women (wear fun clothes) .... and (have interesting hairstyles) .... Mrs Hall (love dancing) .... rock and roll. She is too old to dance now.

  d In the 1960s, Mrs Hall got her first car. She (not drive) .... before that.

26 Write notes about the following things you used to do in the past and why you stopped doing them.

  Clothes I used to wear: *a pink dress – too small!*

  Games I used to play:

  People I used to see:

  Things I used to do with my family:

  Music I used to listen to:

27 In pairs Ask and answer about the things in Activity 26.

  Example: STUDENT A: *What clothes did you use to wear?*

  STUDENT B: *My favourite was a pink dress/a blue sweater. I used to wear it all the time.*

  STUDENT A: *Why don't you wear it anymore?*

  STUDENT B: *It's too small!*

Study functions: commenting

28 Look at the picture. What do you think is happening?

Now listen to Track 31. Were you correct?

29 Listen to Track 31 again. In what order does Nina (the second speaker) use the following phrases when she listens to her friend Anne's story?

Making comments	Exclamations
a I know the feeling.	**c** How stupid!
b That sounds familiar.	**d** Oh, no!
	e Uh, oh.

30 Add the sentences and phrases below to the chart in Activity 29.

I know what you mean. How funny! Wow! Really? No! You're joking!

31 Tell Anne's story in your own words. If you need help, look at the audioscript for Track 31.

32 In pairs Make up a story

Student A: go to Activity 7 in the Activity Bank on page 135.

Student B: go to Activity 26 in the Activity Bank on page 141.

Speaking: building a story

33 In pairs Use the things from 'Linda's' bag to make up your idea of the past twenty-four hours in her life.

34 Work with another pair.

Pair A: Tell your story. Use these expressions to help you tell your story clearly.

> Yesterday, Linda ... First she ... Then she ...
> Next she ... Later, Linda ... Finally ...

Pair B: Listen to Pair A's story. Ask questions if you don't understand. Make a note of the objects they used.

Example: *Sorry, where did she go? Why did she go there?*

35 Listen to other stories in the class. Who invented the best story? Who used all the objects?

Writing: life story website

36 Read the message. What do Kensuke and Lisa want? Why?

Home | Contact us | Links | Help & Information

Remember us?

We're Kensuke Sato (aka Cat) and Lisa García (aka Panther). Kensuke and I both went to The International School in Los Angeles. We are original members of the band The Zoo. After school, Kensuke went back to Japan and I went back to Mexico and life went on. Last year Kensuke and I were reunited through 'Together Again'.
We are getting married next summer! We want to get the band together again to play at our wedding. Did you use to play in The Zoo? Do you want to re-live happy memories? Bear, Rhino and Fox, where are you? Get in touch to share all the old stories!

37 Look at the website again. Which of the following are included?

a names
b addresses
c name of school
d personal information about the past
e details about their career
f the reason why they want to find their friends

38 Do you want to find old friends? Write a similar message for the Together Again site.

a Look at the list in Activity 37. Which of the details will you include?
b Write up the information for the website.

Listening: radio phone-in

tossing the caber

canopying

car rally

extreme ironing

1   **In pairs** Look at the pictures. Answer the questions.

   a What is happening in each picture?
   b What kind of people do you think enjoy each activity?
   c Do the activities have a future in your country, do you think?
   e Are you interested in any of the activities? Why?

2   Listen to Track 32 and answer the questions.

   a What is the programme about?
   b How many people call the radio programme?
   c What activities are mentioned in the radio programme?

3   Answer the questions. Listen to Track 32 again if you need to.
   a What is Keith's hobby?
   b What is the basic equipment for Extreme Ironing?
   c What was Phil doing when he invented Extreme Ironing?
   d What was Phil's favourite sport before Extreme Ironing?
   e What kind of people do Extreme Ironing?

4   Listen to Track 32 again. Copy and complete the advertisement using information from the programme.

Calling all thrill seekers!

What are you doing this weekend?
How about a weekend of Extreme Ironing?

- -

What is Extreme Ironing?

- -

What do you need?

- -

Interested? Here is how to find out more about this fascinating sport.

- -

5 Copy and complete the chart with information from the radio programme and personal information. Listen to Track 32 again, if you need to. Then compare your information with your partner.

	Extreme Ironing	My favourite leisure activity
Where can you practise it?		
What do you need?		
What kind of people do it?		

6 **In pairs** Using your own words:

a Explain Extreme Ironing. Say how it started and where it is done.

b Say what you think of Extreme Ironing. Do you want to do it? Where?

c Think of other possible 'crazy sports'.

Interview another pair. What do they think of Extreme Ironing? What crazy sports do they want to do?

Study grammar: -ing nouns (gerunds)

7 Match the verbs and the nouns.

VERBS	NOUNS
collect	books
go	films
go to	football
play	horses
read	music
listen to	shopping
ride	stamps
watch	television

Can you think of more nouns for the verbs?

Example: play tennis, play basketball etc

→ see 6A in the Mini-grammar

8 Read the explanations and complete the tasks which follow.

1
We often use an -ing noun, or gerund, when we talk about an activity in a general way:

Watching television is very popular in the UK.

2
Some -ing nouns refer to sporting or leisure activities.

Skating is very popular in Sweden.

a Make the verbs you used in Activity 7 into -ing nouns.

Example: watching television

b Make sentences like this with –ing nouns and adjectives like *interesting, enjoyable, boring*.

I think .... is enjoyable/boring.

c Say your sentences to your partner. Does he or she agree with you?

Example:

STUDENT A: I think watching television is boring.

STUDENT B: Do you? I love it.

Reading: things to do

9 Quick reading Which advertisement is about …

a an activity you can do with your hands?
b activities that can help you earn money?
c an activity that tests your fitness?
d an activity that helps you develop your social skills?
e an activity imported from another country?

It isn't just a dance. It isn't just a martial art, like Kung-Fu or Tai-kwando. It isn't just exercise.

It's an art form: it's CAPOEIRA
This exciting activity started 400 years ago in Brazil's Bahia region. Capoeira was originally a type of martial art. Slaves used it for self-defence against their masters, but in its modern form there is little physical contact

… and it's here!

Come and test your fitness and strength.

For more information, phone: 0800 345621 or look at our website: www.loncap.com

10 Take a closer look What …

a can help you make a lot of money?
b can make you feel good?
c comes from Brazil?
d helps you talk to people everywhere?
e is for people with no experience?
f is more than a dance?
g started with slaves?
h teaches you to make plates, cups and bowls?
i teaches you to use your eyes more carefully?

Did you Know?

Your leisure activities can earn you money!
NEW Courses at Tullyhall College:

Photography for beginners
Discover the secrets of a perfect photo, from the moment of taking it, through to printing and the best way to show it. You don't need a good camera – you just need a good eye. Is there a professional photographer inside you? Come and find out!

Website design
How can you share your interests with other people? Where can you meet like-minded people without leaving home? A website opens the door to a world of possibilities. This course can be the start of a money-making career.

Pottery
Pottery is the art of creating containers and objects out of baked clay. Improve your creativity and make beautiful things for your family and friends.

Grab the *Limelight*!

Here's a creative activity that's fun and good for your social life

Limelight Workshops develop your social skills through acting, singing and dancing. Soon you will begin to speak more easily and clearly, and become more confident. You will work and play with a group of like-minded adults – and enthusiastic instructors will teach you.

Limelight Workshops

Just learning: *working together*
Working with a partner or in groups can help you in several ways. First, it gives you more chance to practise using English. Second, it gives you the chance to learn things from other people and third, you can help other people to learn things from you that they did not know before. Take the opportunity when you work in pairs or groups (like in Activity 1) to practise as much as you can and to learn as many new things as you can from the people you are working with.

11 Vocabulary Match these descriptions with the words from the text in blue.

a the ability to make useful and beautiful things
b 100% good
c something like fighting; something like dancing
d to do things you like with other people
e people with the same opinions as you
f they worked for other people. they could not leave because they were not free.
g when you feel good about and believe in yourself
h when you have cooked something in the oven

12 Read the information about these people.
Can you help them find what they are looking for?
Choose a good activity from the advertisements for each of them.

a Bertha Morris is a very creative person. She wants to learn new skills, and she wants to earn money with those skills.

b Bob likes sports but he is very shy. He wants to do some exercise and meet other people too.

c Marie is bored with the classes at the gym. She wants to do something different. She is interested in other people and other cultures.

d You want to do something different in your spare time. You want to find something you have never done before.

Compare your choices with a partner.

Writing: designing a poster

13 Look at the poster and answer the questions which follow.

Are you musical? Would you like to be?

Music workshops for people of all levels and ages.

We run classes for beginners in many instruments, and there's a singing group for anyone who wants to sing.

Saturdays from 9 – 12.30 at Duxton Hall.

For more information ring 17659 39604
www.duxmustart.org.uk

Come and make music! You know you want to!

a What exactly is the poster about?
b Where does the activity take place?
c When does the activity take place?
d How can you find more information?
e How does the poster say 'it's a good idea'?

14 Look at the poster again. Which of the items a – g are in it?

a details about money
b details about transport
c details of time and place
d details of who is involved
e colourful pictures
f something to attract your attention
g something to make you want to do it

15 In groups Think of an activity you would like to organise.

a Look at the list in Activity 14. Which of the details will you include?
b Write information for all the details.
c Write a short paragraph about how exciting/good for you/interesting it is.
d Design your poster. Include pictures and items from b and c above.

Study vocabulary: activities (and where we do them)

....

16 Listen to Track 33. What sport are they playing? Number the sports 1 – 7.

football (1)   tennis ( )   baseball ( )   bowling ( )

golf ( )   boxing ( )   snooker ( )

17 Where do people play these sports? Choose the places in the box. Match them with the sports in Activity 16. Think of labels for the pictures. The first one is done for you.

alley   ~~course~~   court   field   pitch   ring   table

golf course

18 Guess the words the sentences describe. (The answers are in Activities 16 and 17.)

a This course has many holes!
b It's a ring but you can't wear it round your finger.
c You can't grow plants in this field.
d You can't eat your meals sitting at this one!
e This sport has 'singles' and 'doubles' matches.
f There are twenty-two people on this one and twenty want the same ball!
g A ball with holes in it? That's what you need here.

19 Compare activities from Activity 16. What is the same about them? What is different?

Example: baseball, football

You play both in teams. (same)

In baseball you score runs, in football you score goals. (different)

58 unit seven

....

20 Listen to Track 34. Copy the words and number them in the order you hear them, from 1 – 12.

sin sing tonne tongue ran
rang sun sung sinner
singer thin thing

Which words have the sound /n/ as in *none*? Which have the sound /ŋ/ as in *long*?

21 **In pairs** Dictate the words from the list above to your partner…

Did your partner write down the correct words?

Study functions: inviting

22 Complete the dialogue with a word or phrase for each gap.

MATT: Hi Liz

LIZ: Hi Matt.

MATT: Would you like (**a**) .... rowing?

LIZ: Rowing?

MATT: Yeah. Rowing. You know. In (**b**) ....

LIZ: Of course (**c**) .... 'in a boat'. It's just that, well, you have a (**d**) ....

MATT: You're right! (**e**) .... I thought you could (**f**) .... the actual rowing.

LIZ: Oh no.

MATT: No? (**g**) .... ?

LIZ: I'm not (**h**) .... rowing, actually. I'm not (**i**) .... at it.

MATT: Oh, right. Well, how about a walk?

LIZ: I'm a bit tired.

MATT: Or a coffee?

LIZ: Now you're talking!

Listen to Track 35. Did you have the same words and phrases as Matt and Liz?

23 Match the first half of the invitations with the appropriate verbs.

a Do you fancy
b Do you want to
c How about
d Would you like to

1 go rowing?
2 going rowing?

24 Copy and complete the chart with the phrases.

> I'd love to.   I'd love to but ...   I'd rather not.
> I'm not really sure.   No thanks.   Perhaps.
> That would be great.   What a fantastic idea!
> Why not?   Yes, OK.   Yes, please.
> Now you're talking!

Saying yes	Not sure	Saying no

25 In pairs Practise invitations and replies. Use the words in red in your replies.

a Come to dinner.   rather
b Go skating.   great
c Go to the jazz club.   fantastic
d Go to the cinema.   not sure
e Learn Capoeira with me. perhaps

Think of more invitations and replies of your own.

26 In pairs Invite a partner.

Student A: go to Activity 10 in the Activity Bank on page 136.

Student B: go to Activity 27 in the Activity Bank on page 141.

Study grammar: verb + -ing and verb + to + infinitive

27 Do you remember the toys you had when you were younger? Was there one toy you loved most? Talk to your partner about it.

28 Match the toys with the people.

Toys were us

Mary

'I got my first .... for my 6th birthday in 1972. It was a great big ball, filled with air. I bounced around on it all day. My older brother was horrible! He put a little pin through it. Of course the air kept coming out very slowly so one day the ball didn't bounce anymore and my legs touched the floor. He told me that I was too big and fat for it!'

Clive

'I had to spend months in hospital. I lay there doing nothing for days. I hated being there. Then one day the nurse brought me one of those cubes to keep me busy. It was really, really difficult but I did it in the end – and then I changed it all and started playing with it all over again! I wasn't the only one – people bought more than 100 million of them. Yes, the .... was definitely my favourite toy.'

Imran

'My parents couldn't afford to buy us expensive toys. One day, dad came home with a present. Imagine the excitement! But we were really disappointed. It was just a round plastic disc. But that simple disc gave us hours of pleasure. We loved playing with it in the open air. The .... has got to be the most popular toy ever! They have sold more than 200 million in the past 40 years!'

Sally

'My most memorable toy was my .... When I was about 12 those things were really cool. Even older people travelled around the city on them. My sister and I practised pushing with one foot every day. We wanted to go as fast as possible. One day we tried going downhill together on the same one and we had a bad fall. Only little children use them now.'

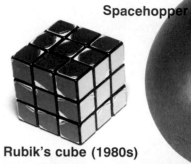
Spacehopper (1970)

Rubik's cube (1980s)

Frisbee (1950s)

Scooter (1990s)

29 Find the following verbs in the text. Do the activities that follow.

| afford start hate keep |
| love practise try want |

a Are the verbs followed by another verb ending in –ing (e.g. doing) or another verb with to + infinitive (e.g. to do)? Copy and complete the chart.

| Verbs + -ing |
| love |

| Verbs + to + infinitive |
| afford |

→ see 12E in the Mini-grammar

30 Complete these sentences about yourself. Use a verb ending in *-ing* or a verb with *to + infinitive*.

a I enjoy .... at home.
b I love .... with my friends.
c I often practise .... in my English class.
d I hate .... at the weekend.
e I can afford .... but I can't afford ....
f My best friend wants ....
g My parents keep ....
h I always try .... other people.
i I have decided .... as soon as I can.

31 Use the following verb phrases to make sentences. Write what you *like, don't like, hate, love,* or *want*.

> dance   eat Italian food
> listen to classical music   ski   study   swim
> talk to my friends on the Internet   watch TV
> work in the garden

Example: I don't like swimming.

32 Compare your answers with a partner. Did you use the infinitive of the verb (for example, *swim*) or the participle (for example, *swimming*) with the same verbs?

33 Copy and complete the paragraph about your favourite toy when you were a child. Don't show your paragraph to anyone.

I got this toy when I was .... I enjoyed .... and I loved .... You play with this toy by .... When I played with it I tried .... I practised .... It is (not) expensive so (not) every one can afford .... Now I want .... Can you guess the name of this toy?

Tell the class about your favourite toy but DO NOT tell them the name of your toy. Can the class guess your favourite toy?

Speaking: a quiz

34 In groups of four Prepare for a general knowledge quiz.

a Look at the different coloured topics. Write three more questions for each colour.
b Each student chooses a colour: orange, yellow, purple, or blue.
c Two groups work together. Students from group A read out their questions for each colour from the cards. Students answer questions for their colour. Check answers for questions a – c in **Activity 11 in the Activity Bank on page 136.**
d Keep a score. Who answered most questions correctly?

Science and Nature

a) What's a herpetologist?
b) What is long-term memory?
c) What is a stressor?
d) ....
e) ....
f) ....

Sports and Leisure

a) What is Capoeira?
b) What can you do with a space hopper?
c) Where can you go rowing?
d) ....
e) ....
f) ....

Geography

a) Where is Glasgow?
b) What's the capital of Jamaica?
c) In what country are French and English official languages?
d) ....
e) ....
f) ....

Entertainment

a) Where's Kylie Minogue from?
b) Give the name of one of the characters in The Simpsons.
c) What is a soap opera?
d) ....
e) ....
f) ....

Feelings

Reading: why do they do it?

1 **In pairs** Look at the photo and the diagram. What is the connection between them, do you think?

2 **Quick reading** Look at the pictures and read the text. Choose the best title for the text.

   a Stingray, the King of Surfers
   b A Danger-loving Person – are you one?
   c The Chemistry of Fear – it's inside your head.
   d A Wonderful Brain

Meet Stingray. He's a surfer. He likes big waves, big, dangerous waves.

But waves like this can kill you. So why does Stingray surf? What makes him look for danger? Doesn't he feel fear?

Dr Ralph Stein is a psychologist. He studies people like Stingray. He says they do feel fear but they are different from other people. And what is different is the chemistry of their brains.

Dr Stein says the differences in their brain chemistry make them do crazy things. 'They do feel frightened, like most of us,' says Dr Stein. 'What makes them different is what they do about their fear.'

All of our brains make an important chemical called *dopamine*. The difference between 'ordinary people' and these 'adventurers' is that they do not have much dopamine. They look for dangerous situations without thinking. But when they <u>are</u> in danger, they feel fear, just like everybody else. Fear (like anger) makes your body produce *adrenalin*. Adrenalin makes the levels of dopamine go up and this – here's the difference – makes the 'adventurers' feel good. In other words, they look for dangerous situations to make their brain chemistry normal.

'People like this need new and exciting situations all the time', says Dr Stein. 'They are usually friendly and confident, but they get bored easily.' And so, like Stingray, when they see an enormous wave, they don't try to get away from it like most of us do. They swim towards it.

3 **Take a closer look**

   a What does Stingray like?
   b Does Stingray feel fear?
   c What does Dr Stein say is different in people like Stingray?
   d What does fear produce in your body?
   e What do these 'adventurers' need?

4 **In your own words** describe why people like Stingray do dangerous things.

5 **Using pronouns** What words does the writer use instead of the nouns in italics? Underline the words.

Meet Stingray. *Stingray* is a surfer.

Dr Stein studies people like Stingray. *Dr Stein* says *people* like *Stingray* do feel fear but they are different from other people.

Study vocabulary: feelings

Just learning: classifying words

It will help you to remember words if you put them in groups. *Word families* are groups of words that come from the same original word (e.g. *jealous*), but have different forms for different grammar/parts of speech (adjective – *jealous*, noun – *jealousy*, adverb – *jealously,* etc.). So when you see a word ask (a) what family does it come from? (b) what is it; a noun or an adjective, etc.? and (c) what do the other words in the family (noun, adjective, etc.) look like? This will help you to remember the word.

6 Find sentences a – c in the text. Who do the <u>underlined</u> pronouns refer to? Choose the best answer, 1 or 2.

a <u>He</u> likes big waves.
   1 surfer
   2 Stingray
b He says <u>they</u> do feel fear.
   1 people like Stingray
   2 people
c In other words, <u>they</u> look for dangerous situations.
   1 levels of dopamine
   2 adventurers

Find more examples of pronouns like this in the text.

7 **In pairs** Do you know any 'adventurers' like Stingray (real or from fiction)? What do they do? Why are they adventurers? Tell your partner.

Example: I think Steve Irwin, the Crocodile Hunter (see unit 4), is an adventurer. He always does very dangerous things. In one programme, he fed a crocodile – and he had his baby in his arms.

8 Match the adjectives with the cartoons.

angry nervous excited frightened happy in love jealous proud sad

Copy the chart. Put the words in the correct columns.

Positive feelings	Negative feelings
To be/feel: happy	To be/feel: sad

9 Match these nouns with the adjectives in the box in Activity 8.

> fear jealousy sadness pride anger excitement love happiness nervousness

Example: *frightened – fear (n)*

10 **In pairs** Talk to your partner about what happens to your body when you have the feelings in Activity 9.

Example:

STUDENT A: *When you feel frightened, what happens?*

STUDENT B: *My heart goes faster and my hands sweat.*

11 Read the situations. How do they make you feel? Make notes.

a You find a big, fat rat in your kitchen.
b You feel a spider walking on your leg in the middle of the night.
c Your best friend stops talking to you.
d Someone you like invites you to the cinema.
e You win the lottery.
f You have to make a speech in English in front of 500 people.

12 **In pairs** Imagine the things in Activity 11 actually happened. Have conversations.

Example: STUDENT A: *What happened?*

STUDENT B: *I found a rat in my kitchen!*

STUDENT A: *How did you feel?*

STUDENT B: *Very frightened. My hands started sweating, my heart beat fast, and my knees shook.*

STUDENT A: *Not pleasant!*

STUDENT B: *No.*

Listening: scary story

13 Look at the picture. Answer the questions.

a What time is it?
b Why is Judy alone in the house?
c What is she doing?
d How is Judy probably feeling? How do you know?

14 Listen to Track 36. True (T) or False (F)?

a That night Judy was looking after a baby.
b The baby was in the room with Judy.
c Judy was enjoying her evening.
d The phone rang three times.
e The first time the phone rang Judy didn't worry.
f The second time the phone rang Judy was frightened.
g The last time the phone rang Judy knew it was John.
h The baby was in his room.

15 Listen carefully to Track 36 again. What were the different feelings Judy had in the story? Tell your partner.

Example: STUDENT A: *First Judy was feeling happy. She was watching a good movie.*

STUDENT B: *But she was crying! You don't cry when you are happy.*

16 **In pairs** What probably happened? Decide on the best ending for the story.

17 Listen to Track 37. Answer the questions.

a Where was Timmy, the baby?
b Who was the man on the phone?
c What does Judy think about it all?

Study grammar: the past continuous

18 Read the sentences. Are the statements a – d True (T) or False (F)?

> Judy **was babysitting** at midnight.
> She **was watching** a film.
> She **wasn't watching** a horror film.
> The baby **was sleeping** in his room.
> The baby's parents **were having** dinner with friends.

a All the sentences have verbs with parts of the verb 'be'.
b All the sentences are about actions in the past.
c The actions in the sentences started exactly at midnight.
d The actions in the sentences probably started before midnight and ended after midnight.

→ see 8B in the Mini-grammar

19 Put the verbs in brackets into the correct form of the past continuous for each gap in this story.

A scary moment

It was a cold winter's night. It (**a**) .... (rain) but it was very windy. I (**b**) .... (sit) on the sofa watching a film. It was really scary: a girl (**c**) .... (babysit) late at night. She (**d**) .... (watch) a film too. The phone rang and a man's voice said: 'Go check on the baby.' This happened several times. The girl ran to the baby's room: the baby wasn't there!

At that moment my phone rang. My heart raced, and my hands were sweating. I picked up the phone but all I heard were funny noises: some people (**e**) .... (talk), others (**f**) .... (laugh), someone (**g**) .... (scream). But nobody answered. I was so scared! A few minutes later I heard a noise: somebody (**h**) .... (try) to open the door!

But it was only my sister. She (**i**) .... (try) to open the door in the dark. I told her about the phone. She laughed. 'It was my mobile,' she said. 'I pressed your number by mistake and I only noticed as I (**j**) .... (park) the car. Sorry!'

20 In pairs Think of your scariest moment. Where were you? What were you doing? What happened? Tell your partner.

Pronunciation: weak forms (*can, and, was*)

21 Listen to Track 38. Are the words in italics *strong* or *weak*?

Mark them S or W as you listen.

a *Can* you remember him?
   Yes, I *can*. I *can* remember him clearly.
b He *was* tall.
   And handsome!
   Yes, he was tall *and* handsome.
c *Was* he there?
   Yes, he *was*.
   What *was* he doing?
   He *was* dancing.

22 Listen to Track 39 and repeat the conversations.

Writing: organising a paragraph

23 Read the paragraph. Answer the questions that follow.

> (1) I just don't understand some people. (2) They don't say what they mean. (3) For example, the other day I was talking to a friend about the salsa class. (4) She sounded interested so I invited her to come with me. (5) She said 'maybe'. (6) When I called her to confirm she made an excuse. (7) She said 'maybe' but she meant 'no'.

  a What is the most important idea in the paragraph (main idea)? Where in the paragraph is this main idea?
  b What sentences give the main idea?
  c What sentences explain the main idea?

24 Number these sentences 1 – 6 to make a paragraph.

> ## organising a paragraph
>
> **main idea**
> ↓
> **(how you feel about it)**
> ↓
> **supporting facts and evidence**
> ↓
> **development of idea**
> ↓
> **(how you feel about it)**
> ↓
> **results, if any**

  [   ] The other day I was at the cinema.

  [**1**] Some people are always talking into their mobile phones.

  [   ] A mobile phone rang three times during the film.

  [   ] I hate this.

  [   ] And the woman answered it every time!

  [   ] I changed seats, but it was really annoying.

25 In pairs Discuss the main ideas below with your partner. What can you write to explain the main ideas? Make notes.

  a I usually feel very nervous before an exam.
  b Why do people like frightening stories?

26 Choose a topic. Write a paragraph.

  a The last time I was really scared.
  b The last time I disagreed with my best friend.
  c The last time I felt really proud.
  d Things that embarrass me.

27 Put a verb from the box into the correct form of the past continuous for each gap in Polly's story.

> work (x2) look up have (x2) do

Polly's story

I am really angry with Laura. Last week we (a) .... a project together. We agreed to meet at my house on Thursday and we started to work as soon as she arrived. Well, when we (b) .... her mobile rang. She made some excuse about helping her father at his shop, and left. When she left I continued to work. But when Sarah saw her later she (c) .... coffee with Joe! I was really angry! While I was (d) .... on <u>our</u> project she (e) .... fun with Joe! And then she phoned on Sunday when I (f) .... things on the Internet, you know for the project, and she says, 'How is it going?' I just said, 'I don't want to work with you anymore. Do your project with Joe.' And I hung up. So now we are not talking. And you know what the worst thing is? I got a C for my project – Laura and Joe got an A!

28 Copy these time lines. They represent time passing. Write the verbs in the sentences b – d above the lines like in a, and show how long the verb was happening

a   When we *were working* at my house, her mobile *rang*.

were working
the past ——————xxxxxxxx———————— now (the present)

the past ———————x—————————— now (the present)
rang

b   She *phoned* on Sunday when I *was looking up* things on the Internet.

the past ———————x—————————— now (the present)

the past ——————xxxxxxxx———————— now (the present)

c   I *was working* on our project while she *was having* fun with Joe.

the past ——————xxxxxxxx———————— now (the present)

the past ——————xxxxxxxx———————— now (the present)

d   We *started* to work as soon as she *arrived*.

the past ———————xx—————————— now (the present)

the past ———————xx—————————— now (the present)

29 Past continuous or past simple? Now complete Laura's story.

> not work hear hang up
> help write not do
> ring talk arrive

LAURA'S STORY

Polly's not telling the truth. First of all, Polly and I (a) .... She was just messing around. We (b) .... anything important. It's true that my mobile (c) .... when we (d) .... Polly was furious! But it was dad, honest! So I did go and help him. I (e) .... in the shop when my brother (f) .... , so I left. I met Joe in the street and we had coffee together. What's the problem? I phoned her later but she (g) .... when she (h) .... my voice. So, fine, I did the project with Joe and she (i) .... hers alone. By the way, Joe and I did really well on our project!

30 Put the verbs in brackets in the correct form: the past simple or the past continuous.

a When Polly .... (hear) about Laura and Joe she .... (get) jealous.

b When Sarah .... (see) Laura, she .... (have) coffee with Joe.

c While Laura .... (have) fun, Polly .... (work) on their project.

d Polly and Laura .... (talk) when her dad .... (ring).

e What .... Laura .... (do) when her brother .... (arrive)?

f Polly .... (get) angry when she .... (hear) about Laura's A.

g Polly and Laura .... (not talk), so we .... (not enjoy) the party much.

31 Have you ever had a disagreement with a friend? Tell your partner.

Example: I got angry with my cousin once. She was staying with my family and she was sleeping in my room. When I came in one day she was reading my diary. I was furious! I told her...

→ See 8A and 8B in the Mini-grammar

Study functions: apologising

32 Listen to Track 40. Match the dialogues with the pictures.

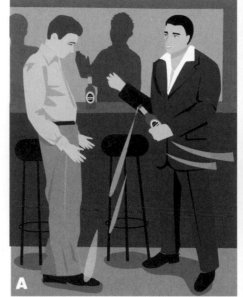

33 Listen to Track 40 again. Which expressions do you hear?

Apologising	Responding to apologies
I apologise.	Apology accepted.
I apologise for being late.	That's all right.
Sorry!	That's OK.
I'm sorry that you waited so long.	Never mind.
I didn't mean to upset you.	Not at all.
	Don't worry about it.

Which of the expressions in the chart are formal and which are less formal?

34 Use expressions from the chart in Activity 33 to apologise in the following situations.

a Your father asks you to help him with his new DVD recorder. You are meeting friends.
b By mistake you hit a woman on the bus with your bag.
c By mistake you delete your friend's work from the computer.
d You are sitting in traffic on a bus and will be late for a doctor's appointment. Phone the doctor's surgery.
e Your friend invites you to stay for dinner. You don't like her food.
f You forgot your friend's birthday party. He/she is unhappy.
g You break a glass in a restaurant. The waiter has to clean up the mess.

35 In pairs Read the situations. Have conversations. Use expressions from the chart in Activity 33.

a Student A, you got home very late last night. Your parents are not happy. Apologise and make an excuse.
Student B, you are the parent. Tell your son/daughter what you think. Think of a suitable punishment

b Student B, you have lost/broken something your friend really loves. Apologise and explain what happened. Offer to replace it.
Student A, accept or reject your friend's apology. Accept or reject her/his offer.

Write down your dialogues.

36 Read out your dialogues from Activity 35 for the class. Listen to the other dialogues. Choose

• the best excuse in a,

• the worst punishment in a,

• the best solution to the problem in b.

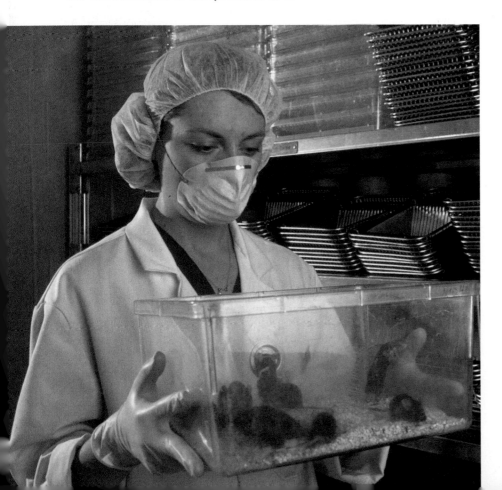

Speaking: animal rights?

37 Read the newspaper article and complete the task which follows.

MICE ESCAPE FROM LABORATORY

Hundreds of mice escaped from the university animal experiments laboratory last night. Police say someone went into the laboratory at about 10 o'clock and opened all the cages and set the animals free. 'This is no joke,' says Detective Glover, 'this was a crime and we are going to catch the guilty person...'

a **In groups**

STUDENT A: go to **Activity 12 in the Activity Bank on page 136.**
STUDENT B: go to **Activity 14 in the Activity Bank on page 137.**
STUDENT C: go to **Activity 17 in the Activity Bank on page 137.**
STUDENT D: go to **Activity 29 in the Activity Bank on page 141.**
STUDENT E: go to **Activity 32 in the Activity Bank on page 142.**

b The Detective questions the other students. Who is the 'guilty person'?

Can you do it?

Listening: phone messages

🔊 1 Listen to Track 41. Choose the correct picture for each of the messages.

message 1

message 2

🔊 2 Listen to Track 41 again. Can you find Debbie, Peter, Melanie, Lucy, Will, Olga or Libby in the pictures?

Now answer these questions:

a Who has a laptop?
b Who left something at home?
c Who apologises?
d Who is going to be late?
e Who's going to buy sandwiches?
f Who's having a party?

🔊 3 Listen to the recorded messages on the answering machines on Track 41. Which is the clearest? Which is the most useful? Which is the most fun? Choose the best one.

message 3

4 Put the words in the right order to make message announcements.

a at / call / can't / moment / take / the / We / your
b a / after / leave / message / Please / the / tone
c can't / come / I / now / phone / right / the / to
d a / and / back / I'll / Leave / message / ring / you
e here / not / now / right / We're

5 Write a message announcement. Share the announcements with the class. Choose the best ones.

Study grammar: *can* and *can't*

6 Copy and complete the chart with sentences a – g.

a We can meet outside the library.
b Can you bring your laptop with you?
c I can't come to the phone right now.
d I can't put a photograph into my computer document – they didn't show me how!
e Can you print photos from your computer?
f I can't read this document – it's in Swahili and I don't speak Swahili.
g Can you play the viola?

Use *can*	Examples
1. to talk about abilities or things people (don't) know how to do.	
2. to say (or ask) if something is possible.	
3. to ask someone to do something.	

→ see 5A in the Mini-grammar

7 Add the following to your chart:

a a sentence about something you are good at.
b a sentence about something you don't know how to do.
c a question you want to ask the person behind you about his/her abilities.
d something to ask the person in front of you to do.

8 **In pairs** Choose a mobile phone.

9 You and technology – how good are you? Copy and complete the chart. Use a dictionary for new words, if necessary. Add two new questions.

Can you ...	Yes/No
put new software onto your computer?	
print photos?	
send text messages?	
burn CDs?	
record DVDs?	
make pictures on the computer?	
mix music like a DJ?	

10 Use the questions to ask other students what they are good at.

Example:

STUDENT A: *Can you mix music like a DJ?*

STUDENT B: *Yes, I can/No I can't.*

a
Sony Ericsson
1.3 MEGA PIXEL

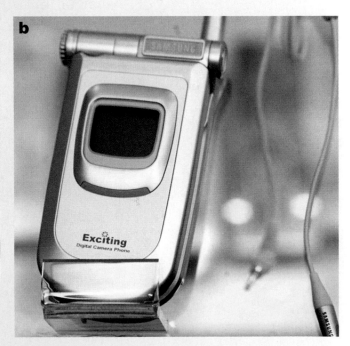

b
Exciting
Digital Camera Phone

If you chose Phone a, go to Activity 15 in the Activity Bank on page 137. If you chose Phone b, go to Activity 31 in the Activity Bank on page 142.

Study vocabulary: phrasal verbs

11 Match the words (a – f) and the items in the picture (1 – 6).

a socket
b headset
c power button
d plug
e volume control
f output

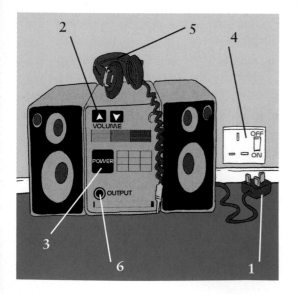

12 Look at the sentences. What do you notice about the words in blue?

Turn on the television. or Turn the television on.
Plug in the computer. or Plug the computer in.
Switch off the printer. or Switch the printer off.

13 Which words go together?

	the TV	the computer	the headset	the light	the radio	the volume
plug in						
switch on/off						
turn on/off						
turn up/down						

14 Give advice in answer to these comments. Use phrasal verbs from the chart in Activity 13. The first one is done for you.

a The music is too loud! *Turn down the volume.*
b I can't hear what the people on the radio are saying.
c I'm bored with this game.
d I can't see anything!
e I don't want everybody to hear the CD.
f I want to watch my new TV. Where do I start?
g I plugged in the CD player and I turned it on but nothing is happening!

Reading: fixing it

15 Do you ever have problems with technology? What do you do about it?

☐ I ask a friend for help.

☐ I read the instruction manuals.

☐ I ask the people in the shop where I bought it.

☐ I get really angry and hit the machine.

☐ I get help online (on the Internet).

☐ I ring a helpline.

☐ Other: (describe) ....

Compare your answers with your partner. Which works best?

16 Read the advertisement. What is it for? Who is Steve?

Are you having problems with technology?

*I'm Steve and I am here to help you.
No problem is too big or too small. Just email your
question and I'll get right back to you. It's that simple.*

steve@teknoprobs.com

17 Quick reading Read Steve's emails. Match the problems and the advice.

A Dear Steve,
I have a large collection of videos. They are very important to me. My VCR is broken and they couldn't repair it. I couldn't find a new one in the shops but I managed to find a combination one (VCR and DVD player). But what can I do when they stop making those too?

B Dear Juanita,
A few years ago you could find second-hand record players easily. Now they can be quite difficult to find. I managed to buy one on the Internet recently. Try one of the web sites for second hand equipment, like www.wozwunce.com

C Dear Steve,
I had some old software on my computer. My friends advised me to buy a program so I did – even though I could still use my old software without any problems. I'm not that good with computers, but I somehow managed to install it but I still can't use it properly. What can I do? I couldn't understand the online tutorial at all.

D Dear Mark,
It's time to change your technology. Choose your best videos and record them onto DVDs. 'Precious moments' on Clarence Road have a special service. They can even add music and commentary to your film!

E Dear Steve,
My father has a valuable collection of records but he can't play them anymore. He prefers the sound of old fashioned vinyl records, so CDs are out. I want to buy him a record player for his birthday. Can you still buy them?

F Dear Susanna,
Get a personal tutor or take a computer class. It's expensive but it is worth it. You can find a tutor in the local newspaper and the local college has lots of computer classes at all levels.

18 Scan the text. Find:

a a good place to record videos onto DVDs

b a good way to learn to use a computer

c a good place to find equipment that is not made anymore

d a problem caused by new technology

e something that can help you use your software correctly

19 Take a closer look Read the emails again carefully. Answer the questions.

a 'They are very important to me.'
What are very important?

b 'Now they can be quite difficult to find.' What can be difficult to find?

c 'I somehow managed to install it …' What did he manage to install?

d '… and record them onto DVDs.' Record what onto DVDs?

e 'I want to buy him a record player …' Buy who a record player?

f 'Can you still buy them?' Buy what?

20 Vocabulary Look at the words in blue in the text. Match them with the definitions.

a to make a broken object good again (v)

b not new and used by someone else before you (adj)

c a set of similar things put together (n)

d worth a lot of money (adj)

e to connect a piece of equipment and make it ready to use (v)

f not modern (adj)

g in a correct way (adv)

h to be able to do something difficult after trying hard (v)

Study grammar: *could* and *managed to*

21 Read the sentences. Copy the chart and complete it with the sentences.

Meaning	Examples
Talking about abilities in the past	My camera broke and they couldn't repair it.
Talking about things that were difficult to do but which, once, you did.	

a My camera broke and they couldn't repair it.

b I really tried hard but I didn't manage to install the software.

c He could use a video recorder when he was five.

d Did you manage to find a record player?

e I managed to find a Beatles record on the Internet.

f Could you use the Internet twenty-five years ago?

g Before my classes I couldn't use a computer properly.

22 Copy and complete the chart with ticks (✓) or crosses (✗).

	could	managed to	could not (couldn't)
We use *did* with the past			
We use *did* for the negative			
Is followed by infinitive without *to*			

→ see 5B in the Mini-grammar

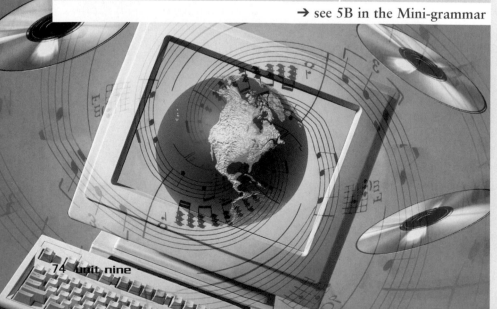

23 Use *could, couldn't, managed to,* or *didn't manage to*, to complete the sentences.

a Jon wanted a new TV. He .... save enough money to buy one with a plasma screen. He is very proud of his new TV.

b At the age of five Rachel .... use a word processor and she .... play computer games. But at the age of 12 she .... multiply or divide without a calculator.

c Matthew .... understand what the problem was with his email. He .... get through to the helpline only after trying for hours.

d Mia's computer crashed but she .... save most of her documents. Unfortunately, she .... save her address book so she .... write to her friends.

e Martha worked very hard but she .... pass her exam. It was surprising because in the past she .... always pass exams easily.

f Rachel's car stopped on her way to work. She .... push it to the side of the road but she .... start it again. She called the garage for help.

g Ollie lost his keys and he .... get into his house. He .... break a window but the alarm rang and the police came!

24 Complete the sentences about Pei-ling. Use *could, couldn't, managed to* or *didn't manage to* to complete the sentence.

Pei-ling is from Taiwan.

a At the age of four she .... read the newspaper.

b At the age of six she .... record programmes from the television.

c At the age of eight she .... speak English well and she .... understand texts in Spanish.

d By the end of primary school she .... do algebra (but she .... ride a bike!).

e In secondary school she .... skip a year at school.

f At 13 she .... beat adults at chess and she .... win an international chess competition.

g Last year she .... pass her university entrance exams but she still .... ride a bike.

25 Could you do the same things as Pei-Ling at the same age? Can you do them now? Tell your partner.

Example:

STUDENT A: At the age of four I could read the newspaper too.

STUDENT B: Could you speak English well at six?

STUDENT A: No, I couldn't then but I can now.

Study functions: making phone calls

26 Put the conversations in the correct order.

a

[ ] Bye.

[ ] Hi Sue. It's Harry. Is Milly there?

[1] Hello.

[ ] No, that's OK. I'll call her later.

[ ] OK. See you.

[ ] No, she's out. Do you want me to say you called?

b

[1] Hello, Language Centre. Can I help you?

[ ] Yes, I'll hold.

[ ] Sorry to keep you waiting. The line is still engaged. Can I take a message?

[ ] Could you put me through to Mr Rose?

[ ] I'm sorry. The line is busy. Would you like to hold?

[ ] Yes. Could you tell Mr Rose that Harry Parker called? It's about his DVD player.

[ ] Of course.

Listen to Track 42. Check your answers.

27 Copy and complete the chart with phrases from the dialogue.

Making phone calls	Formal	Informal
Offering help		
Making a request		
Asking to speak to someone	Can/could I speak to ...? I'd like to speak to	Put Helen on, please.

28 Listen to Track 42 again and read the conversations. Find:

a Two different ways of answering the phone.
b Two reasons why you can't speak to the person you're calling.
c An expression that means 'can you wait'?

29 Complete the phone calls.

1 You are phoning a shop where you bought an MP3 player. It doesn't work. You want your money back.

SHOP: Hello. Best Electronics. Can I help you?
YOU: (ask to speak to the manager)
SHOP: Who's calling please?
YOU: (introduce yourself)
SHOP: Sorry, his line's engaged.
YOU: (ask her to take a message)
SHOP: Sure.
YOU: (leave a message)

2 You are phoning Steve, a friend. You lent him a computer game. You want it back.

STEVE'S SISTER: Hello.
YOU:
STEVE'S SISTER: No. He's out. Do you want him to phone you back?
YOU:
STEVE'S SISTER: Oh, here he is. You can tell him yourself.
YOU:

Listen to Track 43. Compare your versions. Which is better?

Pronunciation: question intonation

30 Look at the groups of questions. Why are they different?

A What's her number?
  How can I help?
  Who's calling, please?

B Is Rose there?
  Do you have his number?
  Can I help you?

Listen to Track 44. Does the voice go up or down? Mark the questions ↘ (down) or ↗ (up). What do you notice?

31 Say these questions with the correct intonation. Mark them ↘ or ↗. Then listen to Track 45 to check your answers.

a Can you help me?
b Would you like to leave a message?
c What time will she be back?
d How do you spell that?
e Do you want her to call you back?
f Who's calling?

32 Practise reading the questions with the correct intonation.

Speaking: what shall we take?

33 Which words from the box belong to which pictures?

> mobile phone   video games   camcorder   MP3 player
> computer   radio   digital camera   three-wheeled motorbike

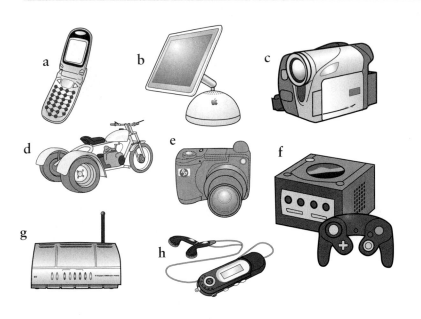

a b c
d e f
g h

34 **In pairs** You and your partner are going to live in Antarctica for two months. You're going to do some experiments about climate change.

a What are you going to take? Why? Choose four of the items in the pictures above, plus one extra item of your choice. Make a note of your reasons.

Example:

MP3 player – can't live without music, it's fun, can take lots and lots of music.

b Compare your choices with another pair.

Example:

STUDENT A: What do you want to take?

STUDENT B: An MP3 player because you can take lots of music.

STUDENT A: We'd rather take a camcorder because …

c Listen to other people's choices. What are the five most popular choices in the class?

Writing: using pronouns

35 Read the paragraph. Can you tell what is wrong with it? Tell your partner.

> Technology drives me crazy because I am not very good with <u>technology</u>. For example, I use the computer all the time but I can't use <u>the computer</u> well. All my friends are surprised because <u>all my friends</u> use their computers all the time. I'm going to take a course and surprise <u>all my friends</u> even more!

36 Replace the underlined words with *it*, *they*, or *them*.

37 Rewrite these paragraphs. Use pronouns to avoid repetition.

a A lot of people hate answering machines but I love answering machines. As soon as I get home I turn my answering machine on and listen to the messages on my answering machine. My answering machine is also useful because I can hear who is calling and only answer if I want to.

b Mariella can't live without her hairdryer. Mariella uses her hairdryer every day because Mariella thinks her looks are very important. Mariella even took her hairdryer when we went camping but the batteries were flat and of course Mariella couldn't plug her hairdryer in anywhere.

38 How do you feel about technology? Write a paragraph. Use pronouns to avoid repetition.

Give and take

Listening: Clayton Street

a

b

1 Listen to the scene from the soap opera Clayton Street on Track 46. Look at the pictures. Which is Jezza? Which is Chris?

2 Listen to Track 46 again. What do you think? Choose the best answers.

a Jezza
1 is a good friend to Chris.
2 is not a good friend to Chris.

b Chris
1 is unhappy because Jezza didn't put his number in the 'phonebook' on his mobile phone.
2 is not happy because Jezza didn't remember his number.

c Chris
1 wants his money back.
2 is going to give Jezza some money.

d Chris
1 is sure that he will get £200 from Jezza.
2 isn't sure that he will get £200 from Jezza.

e Jezza
1 will give Chris £200 tomorrow.
2 won't give Chris £200 tomorrow.

3 What do these verbs mean? Check with your partner.

believe   have got   have got to   get
give   lend   say   show   want

Look at the lines from Track 46. Put the correct form of the verbs in the gaps.

a Where it .... you the number?
b You .... me in your phonebook, haven't you?
c (I) Don't .... it.
d But what do you .... ?
e I .... you two hundred pounds, remember?
f I'll .... it to you tomorrow.
g You .... that before.
h You'll .... your money tomorrow.
i I .... go.

Listen to Track 46 again. Were you correct?

Study grammar: verbs with two objects

Just learning: *finding and using 'rules'*

When you find a grammar rule (in the Students' Book, in the grammar charts, or in a grammar book), the best thing is to use it as much as possible. You can do three things: (a) make as many sentences and questions as you can using the new rule, (b) look for as many examples as you can of the grammar rule in action, and (c) look for grammar words in dictionaries and study the examples there.

4 Look at the sentences and answer the questions.

a She gave a present to Jane.
b She gave it to her.
c She gave Jane a present.
  1 What (= direct object) did she give?
  2 Who received the present (= indirect object)?

Which sentence (a, b or c) is an example of each rule in the chart below?

Two objects: what goes where?

- When we have two objects we often put the **indirect** object first
  Example 1:

- We can put the **direct** object first, but then the *indirect* object needs a *preposition*
  Example 2:

- When the **indirect** object and the **direct** object are both pronouns, the **direct** object comes **first**
  Example 3:

→ see 12F in the Mini-grammar

5 Read these sentences. Which are correct? Which are wrong?

a She gave a present to me.

b She gave a present to my mother.

c She gave it me.

d She gave me it.

e She gave to me a present.

f She gave my mother a present.

g She gave to my mother a present.

Correct the wrong sentences.

6 Put the following words in order to make correct sentences.

a a / letter / me / She / wrote

b bought / for / him / I / it

c a / for / girlfriend / He / his / played / song

d a / birthday / for / gave / me / mother / My / my / radio

e a / cost / It / lot / money / of / them

f a / daughter / her / read / She / story / to

g a / good / He / offered / price / them

h a / father / I / lot / money / my / of / owe / to

7 Who did what? Complete the story using the verbs in the box. Use the past tense if possible.

buy   give   leave   lend   owe   pay
read   send   show   teach   write

Steve (**a**) .... Jim some money and Jim (**b**) .... an expensive present for Judy – a beautiful jacket. Judy was very happy and (**c**) .... the present to her friend Ingrid. Two weeks passed. Steve wasn't very happy. He (**d**) .... Jim an email. You (**e**) .... me some money, he said. Jim (**f**) .... him a text message. '2 bad. U can 4get it,' he texted. Steve (**g**) .... the text message to his friend Philip so Philip rang up Jim and (**h**) .... him a message. '(**i**) .... Steve his money,' he said, but Jim said 'no'. 'Right,' said Steve, 'I'm going to (**j**) .... him a lesson' but then Jim rang him up. 'I'll (**k**) .... you half today,' he said, 'and half next week. Is that OK?' And it was. But Steve isn't going to lend Jim any money ever again!

Write the following sentences with *borrow* and *lend*.

When you .... money you give money to someone (and you expect it back). When you .... money you take money from someone and you expect to give it back.

8 Student A covers the text in Activity 7. Student B asks questions. Can A remember who it was?

Examples: *Who lent Jim some money?*

Who sent Steve a text message?

9 Think about the last time you lent something to somebody – or somebody lent something to you. Make notes about it.

Tell your story to your partner. Use your notes.

Speaking: the best present

a

10 Listen to Track 47 and choose the correct picture (a – d) below.

b

11 Copy and complete the table with two more questions about your partner's 'best present'.

Questions	Answers
Who gave it to you?	
When did they give it to you?	
Do you still have it?	
Why do you/did you like it?	
....	
....	

c

12 Interview your partner about their 'best present' and write in his/her answers.

Example: STUDENT A: What is or was your best present?

STUDENT B: My new digital audio player...

Tell the rest of the class about your partner's 'best present'.

Example: Fahad's best present was his digital audio player. It was a present from his brother last year, on his birthday. He likes it because ...

d

Study vocabulary: giving and receiving

13 What do the expressions mean? Talk to other students or use a dictionary.

a birthday	an engagement	Father's Day	going away
Mother's Day	a religious festival	a wedding	

a What do you give (e.g. presents, money, cards), if anything, for the different events above?

b Do you give cards and presents, etc. on any other day?

14 Match the pictures with the words in blue in columns A & B.

Now match the first half of sentences (column A) with the second half (column B).

A	B
a He changed it	1 a gold watch.
b Peter	2 by credit card.
c Later, Peter took	3 cash.
d Lucy went	4 for her friend Peter.
e She asked for a	5 pay by cheque.
f She chose	6 receipt.
g She didn't	7 to Peter.
h She didn't pay in	8 to the shops.
i She gave the watch	9 wrapped up the watch.
j She paid	10 unwrapped the present.
k She was looking for something	11 the watch back to the shop.
l The shop assistant	12 for something else.

15 Put the events in Activity 14 in sequence.

Example: *Lucy went to the shops. She was looking for something ...*

16 Fill in the gaps in the following conversation extract using only three different words from Activity 14.

A Good morning. Can I help you?

B Yes. My mother (**a**) .... me this present for my birthday and I'd like to (**b**) .... it, please.

A (**c**) .... it?

B Yes, (**d**) .... it for something bigger.

A That should be possible. Do you have the (**e**) .... ?

B The (**f**)............... ?

A Yes, first I need the (**g**) ...., then you can (**h**) .... it.

B Ah, well …

How does the conversation finish? Act it out for the class.

Study functions: thanking people

🔊 **17** Listen to Track 48. Which is the correct picture?

🔊 **18** Listen to Track 48 again. Complete the dialogue.

JANE: I just want to **(a)** ....
CARL: You're **(b)** ....
JANE: No really. You **(c)** ....
CARL: It was **(d)** ....
JANE: No really. Thanks to you it was **(e)** ....
CARL: **(f)** .... a relief.
JANE: Seriously, thank you **(g)** ....
CARL: Sure.

19 In pairs Read through the following phrases and decide whether they are thanks because

1 someone did something for you,

2 someone gave you something, or

3 someone helped you.

   Note: Some of them could be for more than one.

> It's just what I wanted.
> It's really kind of you.
> Many thanks for ....
> Thank you for all your help/everything you've done for me.
> Thank you so much for ...ing ... .
> Thanks a lot.
> Thanks to you the .... was a great success.
> You've saved my life! Thanks.

a What's the difference between *thank you* and *thanks*?
b Use each phrase as 'thank you's' for as many things as possible (e.g. presents, helping with homework/moving house/organizing a party, etc.).

20 Reply to 'thank you's' from Activity 19. Choose phrases that fit the situation from this box.

> Don't mention it.
> I'm glad you like it.
> It was a pleasure.
> It's cool (*very informal/conversational*).
> No problem (*informal*).
> Sure (*more common in American English*).
> That's a relief.
> You're welcome (*more common in American English*).

Example:

STUDENT A: *Thank you for my present. It's just what I wanted.*

STUDENT B: *I'm glad you like it.*

a

b

c

d

Pronunciation: /θ/

21 Listen to Track 49. Which word do you hear?

a	three	free
b	thank	tank
c	path	part
d	north	nought
e	theme	team
f	sings	things
g	sink	think
h	thirty	dirty
i	thirst	first

22 Say the words with the sound /θ/, like 'thank'.

Writing: 'thank you' letters, emails and txt

23 Match the 'thank you' messages to the pictures.

1 Hey, about the party. Great. I'll be there.

2 Hi Carol,
Thanks for invite. I'd love to.
See you tomorrow.
Matt

3 Dear Mr and Mrs Jordan,
Thank you for the invitation to your party on December 23. We would love to come.
With best wishes,
John and Brian

4 Thx 4 invite. I'll b there. CU 2moro.

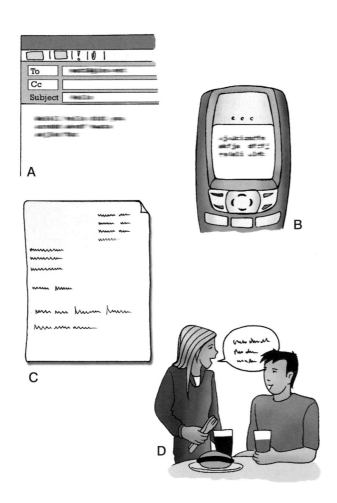

A

C

D

24 In Activity 23 everyone says 'yes'. Now match these 'no' replies to Pictures A – D.

a Can't come. Nxt wk?

b 'Fraid I can't make it. Sorry. See you around.

c I'm afraid I can't make it. What a pity! But let's get together soon.

d I'm afraid we won't be able to come, but I hope we'll see you soon.

25 Look at Activities 23 and 24 and answer these questions.

a When do we say 'Dear' ..., and when do we say 'Hi' ...?

b When do we say 'I'd like'? When do we say 'I would like'?

c When do we write 'with best wishes'?

d When do we say 'won't be able to come'? When do we say 'can't make it'?

e What does '4' mean? What do 'CU' and 'nxt' mean? Why are they like that?

26 Reply to the following invitations. Be careful with formal or informal language.

> Hi Kate
> We're having a party on Saturday. Do you want to come? About 8?
> David

> Can u meet 4 dinner 2moro eve? C

> *Dear Matthew,*
> *I am writing to invite you to a dinner party on Saturday January 15th. I do hope you will be able to come.*
> *Best wishes*
> *Sarah*

Study grammar: reported speech (verb + object + (to) + infinitive)

27 Read the explanation and then say whether the verbs in the box are like A or B.

> ask   order   want

> *To* or <u>not</u> *to?*
> **A**
> Many verbs are followed by an object + *to* + infinitive.
> *The teacher told him* (object) *to sit* (to + infinitive) *down.*
> **B**
> A few verbs are followed by the infinitive <u>without</u> *to.*
> *The teacher let Mary and Stella* (object) *take* (infinitive) *the exam a day late.*

→ see 11B & 12G in the Mini-grammar

28 Mary is 16 and trains every week to be a boxer. She wants to enter a competition. Look at what people said about this in sentences a – h. Match the sentences with these verbs.

ask beg invite order remind tell want warn

a Frank (Mary's trainer): You must enter the competition.

b Martin (boyfriend): Don't enter the competition. Please, please, please, please don't!

c Paul (brother): I'd like my sister to enter the competition.

d Sam Gordon (competition organiser): Would you like to enter my competition? Please do.

e Mr Graham (father): Enter the competition. I'm telling you.

f Sue (her sister): Don't forget to enter the competition!

g Brad (her close friend): Don't enter the competition! It's a bad idea. Very dangerous. Stay away.

h Anita (best friend): Please enter the competition. Then I would be happy.

29 Tell the story using the verbs in Activity 28.

Example: Martin begged her not to enter the competition.

30 Ask students in the class to talk to Mary. Choose the right verbs.

Example:

STUDENT A: Tell her not to enter the competition.

STUDENT B: Don't enter the competition.

Reading: culture clash?

31 Look at the three people on page 85 and read what they say. Are their customs the same as yours?

32 Read the introduction

Alice is reading her emails. Three of them are from three different friends. The friends are volunteers in different countries. That means they are working because they want to, but they are not being paid.

Now read the emails. Say which countries Joanna, Anthony and Naomi are in (look back at Activity 31). Explain their 'mistakes'.

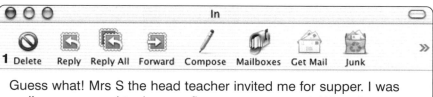

Guess what! Mrs S the head teacher invited me for supper. I was really nervous so I took some flowers as a present. When I gave them to her she looked at them and counted them – I think! Do you think that's possible? Then she smiled and said it was nice of me. But there was something wrong. The dinner was great, though. And at the weekend we're going skiing. It's my first time but I'm really looking forward to it!
I miss you all.
Joanna XXX

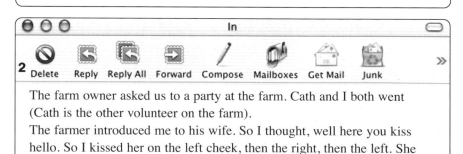

The farm owner asked us to a party at the farm. Cath and I both went (Cath is the other volunteer on the farm).
The farmer introduced me to his wife. So I thought, well here you kiss hello. So I kissed her on the left cheek, then the right, then the left. She didn't look very happy. It was very embarrassing. We talked a lot later and she was very nice. She told me to study Spanish! But I can't help thinking I did something wrong.
But the party was OK. The food was absolutely fantastic.
When are you going to come out to see me?
Love you lots.
Anthony

A Singapore

'When people give you presents you don't open them right then. That looks as if you really need or want them! It's better to wait until later!'

B Argentina

'In my country we kiss 'hello' on the cheek once, but we don't really touch. It's different from France and other places where they kiss two or three times.'

C Poland

'There's this old idea in my country. When you take flowers you must take an odd number (3, 5, 7 etc.), not an even number (2, 4, 6 etc.). Something to do with luck I think.'

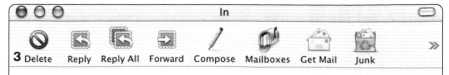

| 🚫 3 Delete | ↩ Reply | ↩ Reply All | ➡ Forward | ✏ Compose | 🗑 Mailboxes | 🏠 Get Mail | 🛍 Junk | » |

It's great here, but sometimes I don't understand things. Take last night, for example. Terry and I invited some people from the medical centre for drinks.

They all arrived at the same time. I offered them drinks, then I gave the wrong drinks to the wrong people. Ouch! But they didn't mind that. Two of them brought us presents. One was a silver key-ring, and another was a really nice pen. But when we opened them everyone looked at the floor. In silence. Imagine! Did we do something wrong? I mean… it was only for a second and the rest of the evening was great fun. Strange. Terry says I'm being silly.

Love to all at the flat. I'll see you in six weeks. Can't wait.

Naomi.

33 Take a closer look Who …

a … cooks really well?
b … didn't say anything for a minute or two?
c … has a nice wife?
d … is a volunteer in a medical centre?
e … is a volunteer in a school?
f … is a volunteer on a farm?
g … organised a successful evening?
h … was frightened?
i … works with Anthony?

34 Vocabulary Find words and phrases in blue in the emails which mean:

a I made a mistake, but I don't know what.
b I'm going to tell you a typical story about last night.
c It's in the future. I'm enthusiastic about it.
d Really, really, really good.
e Something wasn't right. I don't know what.
f They weren't cross or unhappy.
g (You) travel to my place for a visit.
h You keep your keys on one of these.

35 Noticing grammar: reported speech

How do the emailers report the following conversations? Find the reports in the emails.

a Teacher: Would you like to come to supper?
b Teacher: It is nice of you.
c Farmer: Please come to our party.
d Farmer: This is my wife.
e Farmer's wife: Study Spanish!
f Terry and I: Would you like to come for drinks?
g Me: Would you like a drink?
h Terry: You are being silly.

In the sentences in the emails for b and h above, what tense is the verb *say*? What tense is the next verb?

→ see 11A in the Mini-grammar

36 Someone from a different country is coming to your house. Explain your customs. What mistakes can they make?

Before I'm thirty?

Speaking: ambitions

1 All these people were asked 'What do you want to do before you are thirty?' Which of their suggestions would you like to do before you are thirty (or forty, or fifty!)? Tell the class.

I want to visit New York.

Before I'm thirty? I want to climb Mount Everest.

I would like to learn how to fly.

I want to have at least six children.

I would like to play football for my country.

I want to write a novel.

I would like to have my own business.

2 **In pairs** Write a list of 10 things to do before you're 30 for a youth magazine.

3 Compare your lists with other students. Which is the most popular thing to do?

Study grammar: the present perfect

4 Copy and complete the chart with the example sentences.

1 Have you ever visited New York?
2 Has she climbed Mount Everest?
3 He's never written a novel.
4 I've read two books by Hiroki Mayumi.
5 No, I haven't (have not).
6 No, she hasn't.
7 Yes, I have.
8 Yes, she has.

a	We form the **present perfect** with *have/has* + the past participle
b	We change the order of the subject and the auxiliary verb (*have/has*) for 'yes/no' questions
c	We give affirmative short answers using the auxiliary (*have/has*)
d	We give negative short answers with the auxiliary (*have/has*) + *not*

→ see 10C in the Mini-grammar

5 Tell the class about you and the following activities. Which have you never done in your life?

acted in a play	learned to play a
arrived late for an	musical instrument
important class/	played in a winning
interview/meeting	team
been to the moon	sung a song in public
climbed Mount Everest	won a competition
done a bungee jump	written an original story
failed an exam	

Example: *I've never acted in a play.*

Which of the verb endings are regular? Which are irregular? You can check verbs in the Mini-grammar.

6 Ask questions using the verbs from Activity 5.

Example: STUDENT A: *Have you ever acted in a play?*

STUDENT B: *Yes I have. / No I haven't.*

Listening: scene from a play

7 Listen to Track 50 and put the sound effects in the right order. The first one is done for you.

a A knock at the door
b The sound of a mobile phone
c The sound of drinking
d The window crashes open
e Someone closes the window
f The sound of change/coins
g The sound of stirring with a spoon
h The sound of the door handle
i Thunder. **1**

Charles and Miranda pull a bed across the floor. Do they do this before or after h?

8 Listen to Track 50 again. Who (the man or the woman) says?

a It's a bit dark.
b Don't worry dear.
c I loved it.
d I'm not very strong.
e It's scary.
f Nonsense!
g Nothing to worry about.
h Come on. Help me.
i That's better.
j We're safe now.

9 What do we know about:

a the type of hotel?
b the man's and the woman's characters?
c what the man and woman like to drink?
d the name of the hotel?

10 Noticing grammar: tag questions Listen to Track 50 again and complete the following questions from the conversation.

a It's scary, ... ?
b That's better, ... ?
c We're safe, ... ?
d It's not in my bag, ... ?

1 Look carefully at the second verb. Is it a main verb or an auxiliary verb?
2 Look carefully at both verbs. If the first verb is negative, what is the second verb? What is the second verb if the first verb is in the affirmative?

→ see 12D in the Mini-grammar

11 Make the sentences into questions like the questions in Activity 10.

a This is a nice hotel, ... ?
b The water's very cold, ... ?
c They stayed here last year, ... ?
d She likes chocolate, ... ?
e This isn't a very good painting, ... ?
f The water isn't very warm, ... ?
g She didn't leave her bag in the restaurant .... ?
h They aren't going to be late, ... ?

What is the difference between sentences a – d and sentences e – h?

Reading: Caroline

12 Quick reading Copy and complete the chart about the person in the text.

Name:	
Age:	
Occupation:	
Where she does it:	
Favourite music:	
Favourite smell:	

Most actors say that drama school is one of the best times of your life because you act *all the time*. You train and study all day and you often rehearse in the evenings, practising for the next day's show. That doesn't happen in your life as an actor.

When I was twelve or thirteen, one of my teachers – she was called Candy – talked to my parents. She said 'send your daughter to acting school – to a drama school. She's going to be a good actor.' I really wanted to go to drama school too, but my parents said 'No, finish <u>this</u> school first.' And they were right. I got a normal education and then I went to drama school.

I'm a theatre actor. I've done a bit of TV, and I do other things, but theatre is where I feel most 'at home'. But I'm lucky because I don't just act in the theatre, I also direct a schools' theatre group. We go into schools and make shows together with the kids. They help us write the dramas. We do plays about difficult topics for kids. It's easier for them to talk about difficult topics through drama.

Some actors find it very difficult to learn their lines – the words. It's not difficult for me. I don't learn my lines before I go to the first rehearsal. I learn the lines at the same time as I learn how to act the play.

I've never forgotten my lines during a play, but some actors do. I worked in a play once and the actor forgot his lines so he just kept saying the same line again and again. I looked at his face. He was really frightened - terrified! But he remembered in the end. The audience didn't notice anything!

When I'm not working – when I don't have any acting work – I keep fit and do exercises for my voice. My voice is the most important thing I've got.

I relax by listening to music. I like a lot of different music – jazz, blues, soul.

My favourite smell is watermelon.

In their own words

Caroline Rippin, 30, actor

INTERVIEWED BY PETER HEDLEY.

13 Take a closer look Answer the questions.

a Who didn't want Caroline to go to stage school?
b What do drama students do in the evenings?
c What does Caroline do in schools?
d Who got a normal education?
e What is the best time of your life?
f Who learns lines in rehearsal?
g Who wanted Caroline to go to drama school?
h Who was terrified?

14 Vocabulary Match the words from the text with the meanings.

Example: a   *audience*   (6)

a	audience	1	actors have to learn these – the words of a play
b	direct	2	any kind of music or acting event on a stage
c	drama school	3	strong, healthy; can do a lot of exercise
d	fit	4	students learn about acting in one of these
e	lines	5	subjects, themes
f	rehearse	6	they watch a show
g	relax	7	to tell actors what to do
h	show	8	to do something easy; to rest
i	topics	9	to learn how to do something
j	train	10	to practise a play again and again before the first night

15 Talk about these questions.

a Does Caroline have a good job? Why? Why not?

b Caroline talks about 'the best times of your life'. Are they in the past, present or future for you?

c How do you relax?

d What is your favourite colour, smell, noise, etc.?

Study vocabulary: performance

16 Read the paragraph and choose the correct photograph.

Last week I read a review in the newspaper. It was about a new play called *Blue Name*. It said the play was very moving. The reviewer cried at the end, he said. I rang the theatre and booked a ticket. I went to see the play. I got a good seat so I had a good view of the stage. When the curtain went up I was very excited, but unfortunately the play was very boring. It was so slow, and I didn't cry at all! But at the end of the performance everyone in the audience clapped and clapped. So maybe there's something wrong with me!

17 Find words in blue in the text which mean:

a a piece of writing about a play or a film
b it makes you feel very emotional – a good thing
c large piece of material between the stage and the audience
d not exciting
e not fast
f put their hands together
g show/play
h the place where the actors are
i bought/ordered a ticket before the show

18 Look at the adjectives and what they mean.

enjoyable – you like it
funny – it makes you laugh
good fun – you like it – it makes you smile
scary – it frightens you
violent – it has a lot of scenes of fighting and death

In pairs Use the words to talk about a play, television programme or film you have seen recently.

Example: 'The Thing from the Sea' is really scary. In one scene the Thing pushes all these ships out of the way and thousands of people run away. It's enormous and black, bigger than a building and it comes out of the sea and makes it boil.

19 Discussion What are the class's favourite TV programmes, plays, musicals or films at the moment?

Pronunciation: stress and intonation

20 Look at the audioscript for Track 50. Read the underlined phrases and decide exactly how you would say them.

a Practise saying the underlined phrases in the same way as the speakers.
b Practise the scene with a partner.
c Act out a scene for the class.

Study grammar: *for* and *since*

21 Read the information and complete the task which follows.

Carlton Joseph: fashion designer

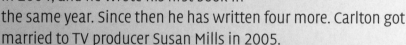

Carlton Joseph is a fashion designer, but not just any fashion designer. He appears on television, he writes books, and he owns his own fashion house.

Born in 1980, Carlton started designing clothes when he was eleven. His father owned a clothes store, and Carlton used to work there at the weekend. Then he did a design course at college.

When he was 21 someone suggested doing a TV programme. He made his first show 'Carlton's clothes' in 2004, and he wrote his first book in the same year. Since then he has written four more. Carlton got married to TV producer Susan Mills in 2005.

Three months ago Carlton started his new company. He called it 'Design: Carlton'.

At work Carlton always wears black trousers and a black top, but at home – or when he goes out – he wears clothes with bright colours (red, blue and yellow). He is especially keen on new glasses – he buys a new pair every few weeks. "I like to look different every day," he says.

Carlton started wearing glasses when he was twelve. He dyed his hair red when he was 18. It is still red, and this year, for the first time, he has grown a beard. "My wife likes it, that's why" is his explanation. But his beard is black!

In pairs Student A closes the book. Student B asks as many questions with When ...? as possible. Can Student A remember?

Example: STUDENT A: When did Carlton start designing clothes?

STUDENT B: In 1991.

22 Read these sentences. Notice when we use *since* and when we use *for*.

Sally has been an actress for ten years.
She's been in the hit show 'Central Park' since last January.

- We use .... with a definite point in time: ....
  six o'clock, ... last year, ... January 24th.

- We use .... to talk about a period of time: ....
  six years, ... three weeks, ... forty minutes,
  .... a long time.

→ see 10D in the Mini-grammar

23 Make sentences about Carlton (see Activity 21) with *since* or *for*. The first one is done for you.

a Carlton has been a fashion designer .... *since 1991* ....

b He's been a TV star ....

c He's had his own company ....

d He's been a writer ....

e He's worn glasses ....

f He's had a beard ....

g He's had red hair ....

h He's been married ....

24 Ask questions about the lives of other students using the verbs from Activity 23. Answer with *since* and *for*.

Example: STUDENT A: How long have you lived in your house?

            STUDENT B: For six years.

25 Copy and complete the chart. Write your own ideas for g – i.

Name: _____	The last time
a see a good film	
b see a good musical	
c meet an interesting person	
d read a good book	
e watch a bad TV programme	
f ride a bicycle	
g	
h	
i	

a Interview your partner about 'the last time'.

Example:

STUDENT A: When did you last see a good film?

STUDENT B: Last Tuesday.

STUDENT A: What about a musical? When did you last see a good musical?

STUDENT B: I've never been to a musical.

b Now tell another student about your partner.

Example: She hasn't seen a good film since last Tuesday, and she's never been to a musical.

Writing: in their own words

26 Think of six questions to ask a celebrity.

Examples: *How long have you been an actor?*

What's your favourite smell?

27 Interview your partner. Use your celebrity questions. Write down their answers.

Example: *What makes you happy?*

– I like talking to my friends, or going on holiday with my family.

What's your favourite smell?

– My father's cooking.

28 Use your partner's answers to write 'In their own words' like the text in Activity 12.

In their own words
Kim Ali, student

I like talking to my friends, or going on holiday with my family.

My favourite smell is my father's cooking.

Study functions: booking tickets, tables, rooms

29 Put the following questions in the gaps in the dialogue.

Can you give me your credit card number?
How many tickets do you want?
Is there anything else I can do for you?
What time do you want to see the film?
Where would you like to sit?

WOMAN: Arts Cinema. Can I help you?
MAN: Yes please. I'd like some tickets for 'The Cuba File', please. For today.
WOMAN: OK. (**a**) ....
MAN: Six twenty.
WOMAN: And (**b**) ....
MAN: Two, please.
WOMAN: (**c**) ....
MAN: Could we have an aisle seat at the back?
WOMAN: Yes I think I can do that. (**d**) ....
MAN: Sure. It's 4552............
WOMAN: OK sir, the payment's gone through. Come along 15 minutes before the performance starts and your tickets will be here.
MAN: Great.
WOMAN: (**e**) ....
MAN: No thanks, that's all. Goodbye.

Now listen to Track 51. Were you correct?

30 Copy and complete the chart by adding items a – o.

  a At the front.
  b How many people is that for?
  c In the middle, somewhere.
  d I think we can do that.
  e I'd like a room for two nights.
  f I'd like to book a table.
  g I'm afraid that that performance is sold out.
  h I'm afraid there aren't any tickets left for that performance.
  i I'm afraid we're full tomorrow.
  j I'm sorry sir. The hotel is full on March 19th.
  k Not too near the back.
  l That's fine.
  m We look forward to seeing you on Thursday.
  n What dates are you thinking of?
  o When is that for?

Function	Examples
Offering a service	Can I help you? Is there anything else I can do for you?
Saying what you want	I'd like some tickets for Dune Warrior V, please.
Asking for details	Where would you like to sit?
Saying it's possible/not possible.	
Getting a credit card number	Can you give me your credit card number?
Saying what the customer should do	Come along 15 minutes before the performance starts and your tickets will be here.
Ending the conversation	
Describing where	An aisle seat ...

31 Use these words instead of the words in blue in activity 30.

a week	room
back	this evening
nights	ticket
restaurant	time

32 **In groups** Write the different questions from Activities 29 and 30 on separate pieces of paper. Put the pieces of paper in a pile. Take a piece of paper. Ask the question. The other students have to reply.

Example:

STUDENT A: (Picks up a card) Can you give me your credit card number?

STUDENT B: Sure. It's 4579 3334 ... .

33 **In pairs** Make dialogues about booking tickets for a film or a play, or booking a table at a restaurant or a meal at a restaurant.

Act out your dialogue for the class. The other students say what has been booked, when, how, etc.

UNIT 12
Making a difference

Reading: the people quiz

1 Look at these pictures. Do you know anything about these people? Can you guess what they have done?

Craig Newmark (1953–)

Ian Wilmut (with Dolly) (1944–)

Wangari Maathai (1940–)

2 **Quick reading** Match the description to the picture of the person it describes.

DO YOU KNOW THESE PEOPLE?

Who are the people described below?

Try our quiz.

1 This man is a biologist from Scotland. The first ever clone of a mammal was grown by him – a sheep named Dolly. As a child he wanted to be a farmer, but one summer when he was working in a laboratory he became interested in cells and animals.

2 On December 10, 1997, this woman climbed into a Redwood tree that is 55 metres (180 feet) tall. Some people wanted to cut the 1000-year-old tree down and destroy it, but she wanted to protect it.

She came down from the tree on December 18, 1999. While she was in the tree (she called the tree 'Luna') people from all over the world became interested in her, because of the way she was defending the forest. She has inspired thousands of people to help protect the environment.

3 In 1995, this man started an online bulletin board where people could post messages on almost any subject in his hometown of San Francisco. The idea was very popular and there are now Craigslists in over 100 cities of the world in North and South America, Europe, Asia and Australia. On Craigslists you can look for a place to live, you can look for a job, you can buy and sell things or you can just post a message and read replies to your message.

4 In 2002, this young chef started a cooking school for young people. The school was for people who were unemployed and had problems in their lives. The well-known chef started a new restaurant and the 'difficult' students at the school were then given jobs there. Every year a group of young unemployed people study at the school. They are all inspired by this chef.

5 This environmentalist is from Kenya and won the Nobel Peace Prize in 2004 for her work for human rights and the environment. In 1976 she started a movement called 'The Green Belt Movement' which plants trees to protect the environment and to improve life in Africa. 20 million trees have been planted since 1976.

Compare your answers in pairs. How did you get the right answers?

Julia "Butterfly" Hill (1974–)   Jamie Oliver (1975–)

Just learning: *scanning*

Sometimes we read a text for general meaning. But sometimes we read because we want to find out specific information – specific details. We call this kind of reading scanning.

When we scan a text we move our eyes quickly over the text looking only for the information we need. We can often do this very quickly. Practise scanning when you do Activity 4.

3 Check that you know the meaning of these words. You can ask other people or look in a dictionary.

> biologist mammal laboratory inspire environment movement

4 **Take a closer look** Who or what …

a was Dolly?
b is 'Luna'?
c is a Craigslist?
d is for people who have had problems in their lives?
e plants trees?
f wants to protect the environment?

5 **Vocabulary** Complete these sentences with one of the words in blue from the texts.

a When you ride a motorcycle you wear a helmet to .... your head.
b He is a great .... The food he makes looks good and is delicious.
c This animal is exactly the same as that one – in fact it looks like a ....
d They want to .... the building because it is dangerous. Now they are going to build a new, safer building.
e Please put your message on this .... Then everyone can see it.
f All living things are made up of ....
g All people have .... These are the basic things that we expect, like the right to live and the right to work.
h I don't have a job, so I am ....

6 **Noticing grammar: passive voice**

Find sentences in the texts that mean the same as these sentences.

a He grew the first clone of a mammal.
b The well-known chef gave the 'difficult' students at the school jobs there.
c The movement has planted over 20 million trees since 1976.

Write the different verb forms in this table:

Active voice	Passive voice
a grew	
b	
c	

→ see 7 in the Mini-grammar

7 **In groups** In your opinion, which one of these people has done the most important thing for the world? Explain your answer.

Study vocabulary: word families

8 Use your dictionary to complete this table with words from the same word family.

Verbs	Nouns
clone	
	protection
cook	
move	
	defence

Nouns	Adjectives
	employed, unemployed
plant	
	interested
inspiration	
destruction	

9 Use the correct form of the words from Activity 8 in the sentences below.

a The young woman was happy to be part of an important .... to save wild animals.

b That woman is an .... to young people today. They see her and they want to be like her.

c I love to try new recipes. What about you? Do you like .... ?

d I have several .... in my house. I have to give them plenty of water and take care of them.

e What do you do in your free time? Do you have any .... , like movies or sports?

f My brother doesn't have a job at the moment, he's looking for ....

g After the storm the beach house was completely ....

h Can you help me to .... this piano? It's very heavy.

10 Look at these nouns. Find words from the reading in Activity 2 that describe people and that are related to these words.

a biology
b environment

Do you know any more words like this that end in –ist?

Study grammar: future simple for predictions and unplanned decisions

11 Look at these pictures and listen to Track 52. What are the missing words in the speech bubbles?

a Oh no! I forgot to buy eggs!
Don't worry. .... and get some eggs.

b .... rich?
Yes, ... a famous writer.

c What time does the film start?
.... the cinema and check.

d Do you think Jamie .... his present?
Yes, of cou... .... He .... it...

Now decide which sentences in the speech bubbles are about:

a a prediction about the future
b a decision which is not planned

12 Choose the best way to complete this statement about the use of the future simple tense.

> The future simple (*will* + base form of verb) is
>
> a only used to make unplanned decisions.
>
> b only used to make predictions about the future.
>
> c used to make unplanned decisions and predictions about the future.

→ see 4C in the Mini-grammar

13 Look at the sentences in bold. Which are predictions (P), and which are unplanned decisions (UD)?

a JOHN: What do you think about the soccer game on Saturday?

MEL: Oh, I think **Chelsea will win.** 1 ....

JOHN: I'm not so sure. **Arsenal will give** them a hard time, I think. 2 ....

MEL: Do you think so? **I'll buy you lunch** if they win. 3 ....

JOHN: OK. It's a deal!

b MADELEINE: Hello. I'd like to speak to the manager, please.

RECEPTIONIST: I'm afraid she's not here at the moment.

MADELEINE: **Will she be back later?** 4 ....

RECEPTIONIST: Yes, **she'll be in the office** by 2 o'clock. 5 ....

MADELEINE: Thanks. **I'll call back then.** 6 ....

c MUM: If you eat any more strawberries, **there won't be enough for tea.** 7 ....

RONNIE: But I like strawberries!

MUM: OK, you can eat those and **I'll buy some more for tea.** 8 ....

RONNIE: Thanks, mum. **I'll wash the dishes tonight.** 9 ....

MUM: You really do like strawberries!

14 Complete these dialogues with predictions, or unplanned decisions using the verb in brackets.

JODIE: Who do you think (**a**) .... (be) at the party?

MARTIN: Here's what I think. James (**b**) .... (be) there, because it's his party. Kristen (**c**) .... (go), because she doesn't like James, and Richard (**d**) .... (go) because he's sick.

JODIE: What do we have to take?

MARTIN: I don't know. I think I (**e**) .... (take) some crisps.

JODIE: That a good idea. I (**f**) .... (make) some dip to go with them.

LAURA: (**g**) .... I .... (make) a good doctor, mum?

MUM: I think you (**h**) .... (be) a great doctor, dear.

LAURA: I'm worried that I (**i**) .... (pass) all the exams.

MUM: I'm sure you (**j**) .... (do) very well on the exams.

LAURA: But (**k**) .... the teachers .... (be) helpful?

MUM: Yes, I think they (**l**) .... (be) helpful and you (**m**) .... (have to) study hard, but you (**n**) .... (pass). I know it.

LAURA: Thanks, mum.

15 Imagine your friend says these things to you. Write possible replies using the future simple.

a What do you think about computers in the future?

b I can't do my homework!

c Have you seen my pen? I can't find it.

d What do you think about the next soccer World Cup?

e Oh no! I've left my money at home!

f What do you think about our next English test?

In pairs Compare your answers.

Example: STUDENT A: What do you think about computers in the future?

STUDENT B: I think they'll become more and more important.

Pronunciation: /əʊ/ vs. /aʊ/

16 Listen to the two words on Track 53.

clone /kləʊn/ clown /klaʊn/

Listen to the words in Track 54 and write the symbol /əʊ/ or /aʊ/ for the sound that you hear for the letters a – j.

a ....

b ....

c ....

d ....

e ....

f ....

g ....

h ....

i ....

j ....

Listen to Track 54 again and write each word out in full.

17 Practise saying the words with the correct pronunciation of the vowel sound.

Study functions: offering to help

18 Match the two parts of the conversations.

a Why don't you let me carry your bags?	1 Thanks. I need to get home early tonight.
b I don't think I can reach the button.	2 Don't worry about it. I'm fine. I ate about an hour ago.
c Would you like some help with your homework?	3 They are very heavy. Thanks.
d Can I help you to finish those forms?	4 Allow me. I'll press it for you.
e Shall I make you something to eat?	5 No, thanks. I can do it by myself.

Listen to Track 55. Were you correct?

19 Now match each conversation with the place where it happened.

Conversation a	at home
Conversation b	at the supermarket
Conversation c	at the office
Conversation d	in a lift
Conversation e	at school

20 Copy this table and put the phrases in bold from the conversations in Activity 18 into it.

Offering help	
Accepting help	*That would be great*
Refusing help	

21 In pairs Offer your partner different kinds of help. Your partner may accept or refuse.

a Your partner wants to study in another country, but she/he needs to fill in some forms in English.

b Your partner is going to cook for her/his boyfriend/girlfriend, but she/he doesn't know how to cook.

c Your partner doesn't want to go to the movies with you because she/he doesn't have enough money.

d Your partner has just bought a new computer, but doesn't know how to use it.

e Your partner is studying for a very difficult science exam.

Listening: radio advertisements

22 In pairs Look at these pictures. What do they show? Use these words to help you.

homeless owner clown volunteer rescue

a

b

c

d

e

Listen to Track 56 and decide which advertisement (Numbers 1 to 5) goes with which picture (a – e).

23 Listen to Track 56 again. Are these statements True (T) or False (F).

1 The Fire Service only fights fires.
2 You can get 20% off when you buy something in the Kenneth Cole store.
3 Battersea Dogs Home has dogs and cats.
4 Friends of the Earth just protects wild animals.
5 You can learn to be a clown at a school.

In pairs Correct the false statements.

24 Listen to Track 56 and complete these statements with the words you hear.

1 When we get a call it could be to a road accident, an air accident or a rail accident or to .... someone from a lift.

2 The shoes and clothes that you give us, we'll give to the ....

3 They are here at the Battersea Dogs and Cats Home because their .... left them in the street to die.

4 We are looking for .... to help us with sending out letters and making telephone calls.

5 Come to the California .... School where you will learn the art of clowning.

25 In groups What do you think about the ways of 'doing good' in Activity 24? Which one do you think is the most important? Which one is the least important? Discuss in your group and put them in order from 1 (most important) to 5 (least important).

Study grammar: probability modals

26 Look at the picture.

Bob   Jack   Terry   Murray   Charles

a I think Terry will win the race.   most probable
b Charles might win the race.
c Jack could win the race.
d Murray may win the race.
e Bob won't win the race.   least probable

Which sentence talks about a prediction that you think will definitely happen?

Which sentence talks about a prediction that you think certainly won't happen?

Which sentences talk about something that is possible, but less likely to happen?

→ see 5C in the Mini-grammar

27 Copy this diary and write five things that you might do this weekend.

Saturday	Sunday
9 am	9 am
10 am	10 am
11 am	11 am
12	12
1 pm	1 pm
2 pm	2 pm
3 pm	3 pm
4 pm	4 pm
5 pm	5 pm
6 pm	6 pm
7 pm	7 pm
8 pm	8 pm
9 pm	9 pm
10 pm	10 pm

28 In pairs You are trying to arrange a time to meet this weekend to do your homework together. Have a conversation to find a time.

Example:

STUDENT A: *Let's get together on Saturday at 12.*

STUDENT B: *Hmm. I may visit my grandparents on Saturday morning. I don't think I'll be back.*

STUDENT A: *What about at 2pm?*

STUDENT B: *Hmm... I might have lunch with my sister. Let's meet at 6 o'clock.*

STUDENT A: *I might be with my friend, John, then. I could meet you on Sunday at 10 o'clock*

STUDENT B: *OK. That sounds good. Where?*

Now get together with another pair and find a time when all four of you can meet. Remember you can change your plans if you want to.

29 Talk about future possibilities and make predictions. Discuss these things.

a people live on the moon
b the problem of pollution gets better
c computers control human beings
d we find a cure for AIDS

Writing: opinion emails

30 Read these two emails to an organisation called 'No Animal Research'. Then read the replies and say who each reply is to, Catherine or Bernie.

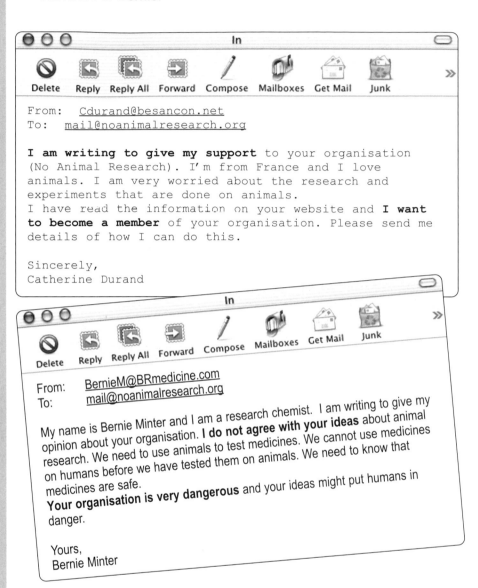

From: Cdurand@besancon.net
To: mail@noanimalresearch.org

I am writing to give my support to your organisation (No Animal Research). I'm from France and I love animals. I am very worried about the research and experiments that are done on animals.
I have read the information on your website and **I want to become a member** of your organisation. Please send me details of how I can do this.

Sincerely,
Catherine Durand

From: BernieM@BRmedicine.com
To: mail@noanimalresearch.org

My name is Bernie Minter and I am a research chemist. I am writing to give my opinion about your organisation. **I do not agree with your ideas** about animal research. We need to use animals to test medicines. We cannot use medicines on humans before we have tested them on animals. We need to know that medicines are safe.
Your organisation is very dangerous and your ideas might put humans in danger.

Yours,
Bernie Minter

a

From: Jenny Morgan [j.morgan@noanimalresearch.org]

Dear _____,
Thank you for your e-mail. We respect your opinions as a scientist, but we do not agree with you. Animal research is not necessary. Please look at our website www.noanimalresearch.org for more information.
Best regards,
Jenny Morgan
Publicity Manager

b

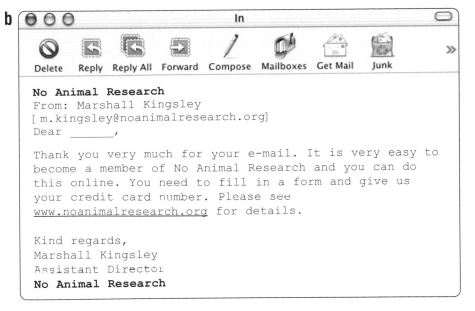

No Animal Research
From: Marshall Kingsley
[m.kingsley@noanimalresearch.org]
Dear _____,

Thank you very much for your e-mail. It is very easy to become a member of No Animal Research and you can do this online. You need to fill in a form and give us your credit card number. Please see www.noanimalresearch.org for details.

Kind regards,
Marshall Kingsley
Assistant Director
No Animal Research

31 Read the emails again. Which of the expressions in bold are used to show that you are in favour of (for) the organisation? Which expressions show that you are against the organisation?

For	Against

32 **In pairs** Write an email to the organisation 'No Animal Research'. Half the class should write in favour of the organisation and half the class should be against the organisation.

You can use the following arguments and any others that you can think of.

In favour	Against
Animals cannot protect themselves – we need to defend them	Humans need animals for food and for clothing
Animals have feelings and feel pain	Animals are not as important as humans
It is not necessary to test cosmetics on animals	Animals do not have rights

33 Now give your email to a pair that has the opposite opinion. Imagine you are a representative of the organisation and write a reply. Then, give the replies back to the original pair.

Speaking: meeting – who shall we ask?

34 Work in groups of five students: A, B, C, D and E. You are at a meeting to decide on one person who you are going to invite to come to speak to your English class.

Jim Garcia

Claudia Barker

Jonathan Singh

Brenda Morris

Student A: go to Activity 16 in the Activity Bank on page 137.

Student B: go to Activity 20 in the Activity Bank on page 139.

Student C: go to Activity 30 in the Activity Bank on page 142.

Student D: go to Activity 35 in the Activity Bank on page 144.

Student E: go to Activity 38 in the Activity Bank on page 144.

Compare your group's decision with other groups.

UNIT 13

Talents and abilities

Speaking: why do we need education?

1 Why do we need to go to school? Match each reason with one of the pictures.

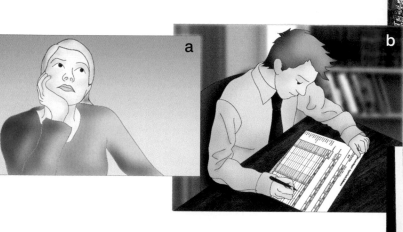

1 To learn about the past.
2 To meet other people.
3 To learn how to read and write.
4 To help us to get a job.
5 To learn about mathematics and numbers.
6 To find out about our interests and talents.
7 To find out about the rest of the world.
8 To learn how to think.

2 Put the reasons in order from 1 (most important) to 8 (least important) for you.

3 Share your order with a partner. Discuss your ideas and agree on ONE order for the two of you.

Example: STUDENT A: Maths is the most important thing we learn at school.

STUDENT B: I don't think so. I think the second one is the most important. We have to learn to live with other people.

4 Get together with another pair. Show them your order and look at theirs. Make ONE order for the four of you.

5 Finally, discuss the statements as a class and decide on ONE order for the whole class.

Example: STUDENT A: Our group thinks that the most important reason to go to school is to find out our interests and talents.

STUDENT B: Why do you think that? We think it's more important to get a job than to have hobbies.

Listening: remembering teachers

6 **In groups** What do you remember about your first school? What teachers do you remember? What did you like? What didn't you like?

Which do you think is more important for young children: discipline or freedom?

7 Listen to Brian and Molly on Track 57. Which teacher did
a) Molly like best, Mrs Gladwin or Ms Marley?
b) Brian like best, Mrs Gladwin or Ms Marley?

8 Listen to track 57 again.

Read the opinions a – f.

Which teacher has each opinion, Mrs Gladwin (G) or Ms Marley (M)?

a Children need discipline.
b Children can stop and start activities when they want.
c Children can discover things for themselves.
d Children of different ages can all work together.
e Children of different ages should be separate.
f Children need to be happy and comfortable.

9 Choose a word from the box to complete each part of the conversations on Track 57.

> strict discipline friendly wild
> ourselves frighten attention

a Remember how she was so .... with us? 'Do this, don't do that' all the time.

b We were all really quiet – afraid to talk. She was really one for .... , huh?

c Ms Marley? Oh yeah – she was great – young and ....

d I was always talking with my friends – the whole class went .... sometimes.

e She never really told us anything. We learned by ....

f Mrs Gladwin used to put us in separate groups so the big kids didn't .... the little kids.

g You know, I think the most important thing is personal ....

10 Which teacher would you like best? Why? Compare with a partner.

Study functions: asking for language help

> **Just learning: *using language to 'buy time'***
> Asking for language help can be very useful for a language learner. It (a) 'buys' you time to think about what the other person said and (b) it means that you can continue the conversation, so that communication does not break down. Don't be afraid to ask for language help; you often understand better the second time!

11 Put this conversation in order. The first one is done for you.

a RACHEL: Oh yes, that's it. A barrister.
b RACHEL: I'm not sure yet.
c JAKE: Oh, it's the study of all things connected with crime and criminals.
d JAKE: No, I'm not going to be a barrister. I'm going to be a criminology teacher. What about you? What are you going to study?
e JAKE: I'm going to study criminology at university.
f RACHEL: Oh, that sounds interesting. So are you going to be someone who goes to court? What do you call it?
g RACHEL: Criminology? What's that?
h JAKE: A barrister?
i RACHEL: What are you going to do when you leave school? [1]

Now listen to Track 58 and check your answers.

12 Match the two parts of these questions to find different ways of asking for language help.

a What does	1 say the study of all things connected with crime and criminals in English?
b What do you	
c How do you	
d What do you call	
e What's	2 the study of things connected with crime?
f Criminology?	3 criminology?
	4 criminology mean?
	5 What's that?
	6 mean by criminology?

13 Match the questions and answers.

a What does 'separate' mean?
b What do you mean by 'grumpy'?
c How do you say that someone knows how to do a job?
d What's a 'profession'?
e What do you call that thing men wear around their necks?
f Court? What's that?

1 She or he is 'trained'
2 A place where there is a judge and you go there if you do something wrong
3 A tie
4 Not together, in different places
5 Not happy, angry or in a bad mood
6 A job, for example, being a teacher

Take turns to ask and answer the questions.

14 Match a word or expression with a definition.

a strict
b uniform
c shy
d popular
e discipline
f discover

1 well-liked by many people
2 nervous with other people
3 order, structure, lack of freedom
4 clothes which show you belong to a group
5 to find something out by trying it
6 tough, having strong rules

In pairs Practise asking for and giving language help using the expressions above and from Activity 13.

Examples: *How do you say that you are nervous with other people?*

What does 'strict' mean?

Vocabulary: abilities and talents

15 Look at these people and what they are doing.

Find the name of the person who has each of these talents or abilities.

a .... is very **sporty**. She loves sports, especially basketball and volleyball and she's very good at them.
b .... is very **practical**. She does all the things that need doing around the house.
c .... is so **creative**. He can make anything into something else.
d .... likes to meet people at parties. He's very **sociable**
e .... has 'green fingers'. Any plant in her garden grows.
f .... is very good at listening and helping his friends. He's an **understanding** person.

16 Write the name of someone you know who:

a can draw or paint.
b can make things with wood.
c is a good actor.
d can read a map.
e is good at growing things.
f makes friends easily.
g is good at sports.
h is a good dancer.
i can fix things in the home.
j can solve problems and puzzles.

In groups Ask and answer questions about the people you know.

Example:

STUDENT A: Who do you know who can paint?

STUDENT B: My mother. She is very artistic. She draws pictures and she sometimes paints.

STUDENT C: What does she draw?

Study grammar:
going to
··

17 Look at these sentences about Jodie and say whether they refer to something that happened in the past (past), a situation in the present (present) or a plan for the future (future).

a Last year I went to France for a year.
b Next year I'm going to go to Russia to learn Russian.
c At the moment I'm studying French at night school.
d My family and I are going to buy a new house this year.
e I've never been to Russia before.
f My friends work in that school over there.
g I'm not going to be a teacher, I'm going to be a translator.

→ see 4A in the Mini-grammar

18 Write your plans for the future.

a This evening:
b Next week:
c Next year:
d When you finish this English course:
e For your next vacation:

In pairs Now ask and answer questions with your partner about what they have written. You must ask at least two questions about everything they have written.

Example:

STUDENT A: What are you going to do this evening?

STUDENT B: I'm going to watch TV.

STUDENT A: What are you going to watch?

STUDENT B: CSI: Miami.

STUDENT A: Who are you going to watch it with?

STUDENT B: My brother.

19 Look at the picture of these students in a school. This person is interviewing them for a TV programme about young people today. He is asking them about their future plans. What do you think they are going to say?

Student A: go to Activity 18 in the Activity Bank on page 138.

Student B: go to Activity 33 in the Activity Bank on page 143.

Take turns to be the interviewer and the students.

Pronunciation: *going to* and *gonna*

🔊 **20** Listen to Track 59. Do the two questions sound the same or different?

🔊 **21** Now listen to Track 60. For a – d below, write 1 if you hear *going to* or 2 if you hear *gonna*.

  a What are you going to do when you leave school?
  b I think I'm going to stay at home tonight. I'm tired.
  c Well, first I'm going to get my doctorate, then I'm going to live in South America.
  d She's not going to be there, I'm afraid. She's going to be in the library.

  Practise saying the sentences in the same way as on Track 60.

Reading: different ways to be intelligent

22 **In groups** What does it mean to be intelligent? Look at these pictures of famous people. Are they (or were they) intelligent? In what way?

Jane Goodall: primatologist

David Beckham: soccer player

Albert Einstein: physicist

William Shakespeare: writer

Oprah Winfrey: talk show host

Frank Lloyd Wright: architect

Anne Frank: diarist

Rev. Martin Luther King: spiritual leader

Ludwig van Beethoven: composer

Who is the most intelligent person you know?
Why do you say that person is intelligent?

23 Quick reading

Read this article about different types of intelligence and match the name of the intelligence to the pictures of the people in Activity 22.

It's not 'how clever are you?', it's 'how are you clever?'

This week's article looks at a great theory and gives you the chance to find your own talents and what you could study. Read on ...

In 1983, Dr Howard Gardner first said that there is more than one way to be intelligent. Dr Gardner says that we all have a lot of different intelligences – *Multiple* Intelligences. Read on and find out what those intelligences are.

- Are you good at learning languages? Do you love to read and write? If the answer is yes to these two questions, you have high linguistic intelligence; the ability to use language.

- What about numbers? Are you quick at doing sums? If so, you probably have high logical–mathematical intelligence – the talent for understanding logic and for using numbers.

- Do you see things in your head? No, you're not crazy, but you probably do have high spatial intelligence. You are probably good at reading maps and understanding diagrams. You probably also remember things using images, colours and pictures.

- How are you on the dance floor? Are you good at sports and dancing? Kinesthetic intelligence is the talent for using your body well to move or to show emotion.

- Do you sing in the shower? Play any musical instruments? Yes? You probably have high musical intelligence – the ability to hear, recognise and remember music.

- Do you love working in teams? Do you have a lot of friends? You probably have high interpersonal intelligence. This is the talent for understanding other people's thoughts and feelings.

- Do you keep a diary? Do you think about your own character and actions a lot? You may have high intrapersonal intelligence. This means you are good at understanding yourself and are self-aware.

- 'To be or not to be' – this is the question for those with high existential intelligence: this is about being able to understand things that are spiritual and things that relate to the meaning of life and death.

And finally:

- Do you like to spend time with nature? Do you have pets? Do you like to grow plants? If so, you probably have high naturalistic intelligence – the talent for understanding how natural things in the world work.

So, how are you intelligent? We hope this article has helped you to find out.

24 Take a closer look
Read the descriptions of the nine intelligences again. Which ones describe you and which ones do not describe you? You can choose as many as you want.

Compare your answers in groups and give examples for your ideas.

Example: I have high linguistic intelligence. I love to read novels and I keep a diary. I also have high spatial intelligence because I'm good at reading maps and understanding diagrams.

25 Copy and complete this chart of word families using words from the text. The first one is done for you.

Noun	Adjective
a language	linguistic
b logic	
c mathematics	
d space	
e kinesthetics	
f music	
g person	
h existence	
i nature	

Study grammar: *will* and *going to* to talk about plans and intentions

26 Listen to Track 61 and write the words you hear for the gaps in these conversations. Use the correct form of *will* or *going to*.

Conversation 1

MARTINA: What **a)** .... you .... do in the summer?

CARL: Well, I think **b)** I' .... be able to get a job at my uncle's shop.

MARTINA: **c)** .... you .... go on holiday?

CARL: No, **d)** I' .... save as much money as I can, because **e)** Kevin and I .... spend six months in Australia next year.

MARTINA: That's great. **f)** You' .... love it there. It's a great country.

Conversation 2

CANDY: Do you think **(g)** you' .... pass your final exams?

JIMMY: Well, **h)** I' .... be really angry if I don't, because I've worked really hard this term. **i)** I' .... work for a top law firm.

CANDY: **j)** .... you still get the job if you fail your exams?

JIMMY: Oh, **k)** I .... fail my exams.

CANDY: It's good that you're so confident.

27 Which verbs in Activity 26 talk about planned intentions and which verbs talk about predictions?

→ see 4A, 4B and 4C in the Mini-grammar

28 Read Marla's schedule and make sentences about her future plans.

MONDAY	THURSDAY
Get to work early (meeting at 7 am) Lunch with James Crawford 1 pm Gym 6 - 7 Movies 8 pm	Report for Helen (7 am) Lunch with Helen Gym 6 - 7 pm Dinner with Harry (8 pm)
TUESDAY	
Meeting at 8 am Lunch with client 12.30 Karate class 7 - 8 Dinner with Sue 9 pm	FRIDAY Breakfast meeting 8 am Work late (- 9 pm) Drinks with Sue and Helen
WEDNESDAY	
Meeting at 8 am Lunch with mum Meeting 7 - 9 pm Jane's birthday party 10 pm	SATURDAY SUNDAY

Example: She's going to go to work early on Monday.

Now make predictions about her weekend.

Example: I think she'll sleep until 10 am on Saturday.

29 Find someone who...

a is going to go on holiday this year.

b thinks she/he will pass this English course.

c is going to continue studying English.

d will probably stay in tonight.

e is going to change jobs soon.

Writing: writing about myself

30 Read what Carmen wrote about herself on her application to a college.

Please tell us about yourself here:

I think I am a sociable, confident person. I get on well with other people and I have a lot of close friends. I love to work with others and I also love animals. I grew up with animals, because my father is a vet and my mother breeds dogs.

I am a very active person and I have a lot of outdoor hobbies, like walking and climbing. I also love playing sports, especially volleyball and hockey, and I love dancing. I play the piano and sing in a choir.

My other hobby is travelling. Last year I visited South America for a month and this year I'm going to go to India for the first time. I enjoy travel because it gives me the chance to meet other people and to get to know other cultures.

Are the following statements true (T) or false (F) about what Carmen wrote?

a She does not have many friends.
b Her parents both work with animals.
c Carmen likes to be outside.
d She is a musical person.
e She has been to India.

31 Which question is answered by which paragraph?

a Why does Carmen like to visit other places?

b What is Carmen like?

c What are Carmen's main hobbies?

What do you think Carmen is going to study? Why?

32 Now write about yourself in the same way. Divide your writing into clear paragraphs, like Carmen's.

UNIT 14
Describing things

Speaking: what is it like?

1 **In pairs** Look at the pictures and discuss the following questions:

   a What does each picture show?
   b What do you think people do there?
   c Would you like to go there? Why? Why not?

   To find out what each building is, go to Activity 13 in the Activity Bank on page 137.

2 Choose one of the buildings. Don't tell anyone else.

   Describe the building in your own words. Can everyone guess which building it is?

   Example:

   STUDENT A: Well it's a modern building. I don't like it very much. It's rather ugly. It looks like a monster's face, with one eye and a mouth.
   But some people think it is beautiful, I imagine.

   STUDENT B: Is it Building 2?

   Useful phrases

   It looks like a ... [+ noun]
   It looks ... [+ adjective]

   Useful adjectives

   big cold dramatic exciting friendly
   modern tall ugly unfinished

3 Discuss which building

   a you like best.
   b will still be here in 100 years' time.

Building 1

Building 2

Building 3

Building 4

Reading: Zaha Hadid

Name:

Country of origin:

Occupation:

Type of character (in your own words):

4 Quick reading Look at the 'Firsts' webpage. Copy the chart and then complete it as quickly as possible.

FIRSTS
Who is Zaha Hadid? by Peter Hedley

Click images for an expanded view

What does a famous architect look like? Well he's normally quite old with white hair. He often looks rather serious. Sometimes he wears modern glasses (the latest fashion), and grey suits. He comes from England, the USA, Germany, Japan or Spain.

But not Zaha Hadid. Firstly, she's a woman. And then she grew up in Iraq before she went to London as a student. Zaha, who is not a quiet person, is passionate about what she does. In the words of writer Christopher Hawthorne, she is 'a big woman with a bigger intellect and a gigantic personality'. She wears fashionable clothes, bright shiny jewellery, and very high-heeled shoes. When she's excited she rolls her eyes, and shouts at the students and colleagues who work with her. But the same colleagues and friends say that she is 'good with people'; it's just that she cares, really cares about architecture. As one of her friends says, when you get to know Zaha Hadid, you realize that all the storms are on the outside – the weather may be bad the other side of the window, but in the house it's all calm and peaceful!

The Vitra Fire Station in Germany, one of Zaha Hadid's first public buildings

But it hasn't always been easy for Zaha Hadid. In 1994, she won a competition for a new opera house in Cardiff, Wales (UK). The public weren't interested, however. They said they wanted a new sports stadium, not the opera house and so her design (see picture) was never built. But other people were noticing her work and suddenly she was designing buildings all over the world (like the Museum of Contemporary Art in Cincinnati, USA) and winning prizes.

In the newspapers they call Zaha the 'diva of contemporary architecture' – as if she was a bad-tempered opera star. Zaha Hadid's reply? 'Would they call me a diva if I was a guy?'

A model for the Cardiff opera house. They never built it!

Home | people A – Z | back to the top | Today's news | Contact us | Help

5 Vocabulary Find the words in blue which mean:

a a place for public football, athletics, etc.
b a very successful female singer, easily annoyed
c easily annoyed
d is really interested in something and wants it to be good
e making drawings and pictures for new buildings
f modern, of the present time
g moves her eyes around to show that she is not happy
h very, very big
i when you can understand things and think cleverly
j with very strong feelings or ideas about something

6 Take a closer look Read the text again and answer the following questions.

a Why is Zaha Hadid different from other architects? (Think of at least three reasons.)
b Where did Zaha Hadid study?
c What is Christopher Hawthorne's opinion of Zaha's intelligence and personality?
d How do we know that Zaha Hadid is passionate?
e What did Zaha Hadid win, and what happened next?

7 Role-play Write four interview questions for Zaha Hadid. You can ask about anything (for example, what she likes, what she eats, what buildings she is going to design).

One student is Zaha Hadid. The class interview her. The student imagines her answers.

Study grammar: *a, an* and *the*

8 Match the explanations (a – h) with examples (1 – 8) from the text about Zaha Hadid on page 111.

a We use *a* to talk about one of something
b We use *an* if the next word starts with a vowel sound
c We use *the* with some country names with more than one word or which end with '... of something' (e.g. The People's Republic of China)
d We use *the* when we mention something for the second time
e We use *the* when we talk about a special thing (or things) that we all know about
f We don't use *a, an* or *the* for the names of most countries (or cities)
g We don't use *a, an* or *the* with plural nouns which describe things in general
h We don't use *a, an* or *the* when we talk about uncountable nouns

1 an even more gigantic personality
2 she grew up in Iraq
3 she wears bright shiny jewellery
4 she's a woman
5 she's good with people
6 the opera house
7 the storms are on the outside
8 the USA

→ see 2A – 2C in the Mini-grammar

9 Put *a, an, the* or nothing in the gaps in the following sentences.

a Magda comes from .... Poland. She lives in .... Warsaw.
b She's .... actress and does most of her work on .... national radio station.
c Her house is full of .... modern furniture, except for .... furniture in her dining room. That's very 'brown' and old.
d .... Polish people love Magda, and now she is working for .... international radio station.
e .... fan (a member of the public who likes her) wrote her .... letter. .... letter was very long, but Magda likes .... letters like that.
f Last summer she went on holiday in .... West Indies.
g She visited .... different islands, but didn't have time to see them all.
h Next month Magda is going to .... United States. She wants to work in .... films there.
i '.............. film industry is very important in .... America,' she says. 'I have .... dreams, but .... big dream of my life is to be a Hollywood actress!'

10 Make sentences using the following nouns to talk about things in general.

Examples: People from Mexico speak Spanish

> (modern) architecture   war   architects
> chocolate   clothes   holidays
> people from (name of a country)

11 Can you make sentences or questions about the items in Activity 10 using *a, an* or *the*? You can look back at Activity 8 to help you.

Examples: There was a war in ...... fifty years ago.

Do you like the clothes in that shop?

Study vocabulary: describing size and dimensions

12 Use the words from the pictures of spiders to tell the class about something you have or know about.

Example: *I've got this new mobile phone. It's tiny.*

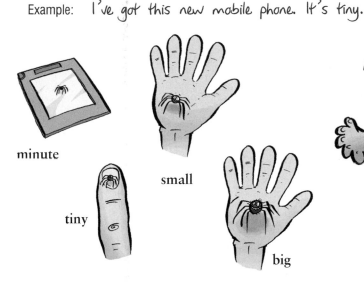

minute

tiny

small

big

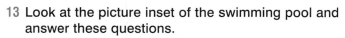

large

huge

enormous

gigantic

13 Look at the picture inset of the swimming pool and answer these questions.

a Which words in the picture are the opposite of low, narrow, and short?
b Which words are used to describe 'thin' things (buildings, trees, etc.)?
c Which words are used to describe 'wide' things (mountains, walls, ceilings etc.)?
d Which words can describe rivers, lakes and oceans?
e Which words can be used for rooms or houses?

Use the words to talk about your room, your house, and rivers, buildings and mountains, etc., near where you live.

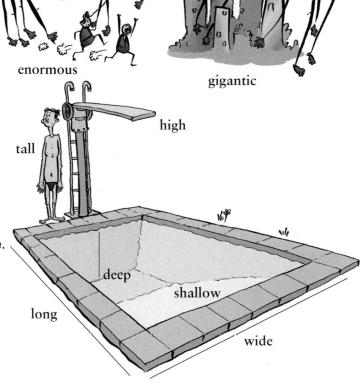

tall

high

deep

shallow

long

wide

14 Look at the pictures on page 114. Ask questions about the pictures using *how* + the adjectives in the box. Guess the answers.

| deep | high | long | tall | wide |

Example: STUDENT A: *How long is the Great Wall of China?*

STUDENT B: *I'm not sure. About a thousand miles long, I guess.*

Now go to Activity 19 in the Activity Bank on page 138. Are the answers there? Who was closest?

The Great Wall of China

The Matterhorn, Switzerland

The Petronas Towers, Kuala Lumpur

The Mississippi River, USA

The Pacific Ocean

The 9th of July Avenue, Buenos Aires

The Witwatersrand gold mine, South Africa

The River Thames, England

Study grammar: superlative adjectives

15 Look at the pictures, and then copy and complete the grammar chart on the next page with words from the pictures (the first one is done for you).

The fastest runner in the race.

The biggest building in the street.

The most expensive car in the showroom.

The cleverest/most clever student in the university.

The noisiest person on the train.

The best design in the fashion show.

How to make superlative adjectives

a One syllable adjectives:
add -*est* fast – fastest

b One syllable adjectives with vowel + 1 consonant:
double the consonant + -*est*
.... – ....

c One syllable adjective ending with -y:
change *y* to *i* + *est* .... –
....

d Two syllable adjectives:
usually add -*est* .... –
..............., but sometimes *most* + adjective .... – ....

e Longer adjectives:
most + adjective .... –
....

f Some adjectives are just 'different': .... – ....

→ see 1C in the Mini-grammar

16 Make the following into superlative adjectives.

bad
boring
cheap
cramped
deep
expensive
fast
fat
funny
good
high
interesting
long
narrow
spacious
thin
ugly
uncomfortable

17 Look through columns A – D. Are there any words you don't understand? Check with a partner. Use a dictionary if necessary.

A	B	C	D
bad	actor		films
beautiful	building		television
big	lake		the music charts
boring	mountain		the radio
(un)comfortable	music	in	the world
deep	painting		town
funny +	person +		your family +
good	programme	on	your house
interesting	river		your neighbourhood
narrow	room		
short	singer		
small	street		
tall			
ugly			
wide			

Ask people about things using words from boxes A, B, C and D.

Example:

STUDENT A: What's the narrowest street in your neighbourhood?

STUDENT B: I'm not sure. Probably Marshall Street, where my grandmother lives.

Pronunciation: echo stress

18 Read the conversation. Which words are stressed?

What's the best film you've ever seen?
– I don't know. What's the best film you've ever seen?

Listen to Track 62. Do the speakers agree with you?

19 Listen to Track 63 and underline the stressed syllables

a Are you happy?
  – Yes I am. What about you?
b Do you like chocolate?
  – Yes I do. Do you like chocolate?
c Have you ever been to the North Pole?
  – No I haven't. Have you ever been to the North Pole?
d Did you go to the meeting yesterday?
  – No I didn't. Did you go to the meeting?

20 Say the exchanges in the same way as the speakers on Track 63.

Study functions: comparing experiences

21 Complete the dialogue with words from the box.

about	difficult	easy	film
know	right	something
sure	think	too

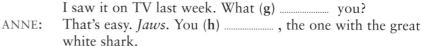

ANNE: Can I ask you (a) .... ?
CATH: (b) ....
ANNE: What's the best (c) .... you've ever seen?
CATH: That's (d) ....
ANNE: Sorry.
CATH: No, that's all (e) ....
        The best film? I (f) .... it's *The Usual Suspects*.
        I saw it on TV last week. What (g) .... you?
ANNE: That's easy. *Jaws*. You (h) .... , the one with the great white shark.
CATH: Yes, I liked that (i) ....
ANNE: I've seen it about fifteen times!

Now listen to Track 64. Were you correct?

22 Practise saying the dialogue. Can you do it from memory?

23 How would the dialogue be different if you spoke the following lines?

a That's easy
b Wait a minute. I'll have to think.
  – Take your time.
c It was definitely ......
d I don't know
e That's impossible

24 Make questions, using the noun phrases with appropriate verbs.

Noun phrases	Verbs
beautiful/ugly thing	been to
delicious/horrible food	eaten
enjoyable/boring book	had
frightening experience	read
good/bad concert	seen

Example: *What's the most beautiful thing you've ever seen?*

Listening: the news

25 Listen to Track 65. Which people and things are mentioned?

airport	queen
car crash	rivers
dog	storms
egg	student
mountains	the environment
nurses	tower
Prime Minister	

Antonia Merritt
Mike Gartside
Phyllis Jones
Stephen Williams

26 Match the names with the people and things you found in Activity 25.

27 Who or What...?

a barked and barked?
b designed a new building?
c doesn't have a job?
d fell in her house?
e is going to be an Egyptian queen in a new film?
f likes architects?
g talked to the police?
h thanked doctors?
i thanks her dog?
j visited a new building?
k was at a press conference?
l won a prize?

28 **In groups** Think of three recent news stories. Write them as news items for radio or TV. Read your stories to the class like a newsreader.

Writing: descriptive paragraph

29 Look at the picture of the 'Swiss Re' building in London. Read the three descriptions. Which one describes the building in the picture?

a One of the most beautiful buildings in London is .... It is two hundred and fifty years old. It is tall and white. It looks very peaceful, and it is a friendly building. Every time I go there I feel happy.

b One of the most exciting sights in London is .... It was built in 2004. It is tall and very dramatic. You can see it from miles away. It looks like a gigantic vegetable, and so some people call it 'the Gherkin'.

c One of the ugliest buildings in London is .... It is only a few years old. It is wide and rather fat. It looks like a tomato. It's next to some beautiful old buildings, so it doesn't look right.

30 Look at each paragraph, and find sentences about:

a age
b description
c extra information
d general opening sentence

31 Find information (and photographs) about a building you like or hate. Make notes about it using the following headings.

How old it is.
Where it is.
What's special about it (very old, very new, beautiful, ugly, etc.).
What it looks like.
How you feel about it.
Any other information about it.

32 Use the paragraph structure chart below to write a paragraph about your building. You can use the sample language in the chart and find more from Activity 31.

Paragraph Structure	Sample language
General opening sentence ▼	One of the .... buildings in .... is ....
Facts about the building (age, etc.) ▼	It is .... years old. It was built in ....
What it looks like ▼	
What I think about it	

A healthy mind and a healthy body

Study vocabulary: the head and face

1 **Look at these pictures and label them with these words. Use a dictionary if necessary.**

nostril brain forehead
tongue neck chin
eyeball lips eyebrow
teeth earlobe eyelashes
hair

2 **In pairs Take turns to give commands when the other person has their book closed. When you don't know the word, change roles.**

Example:

STUDENT A: *Touch your chin.*

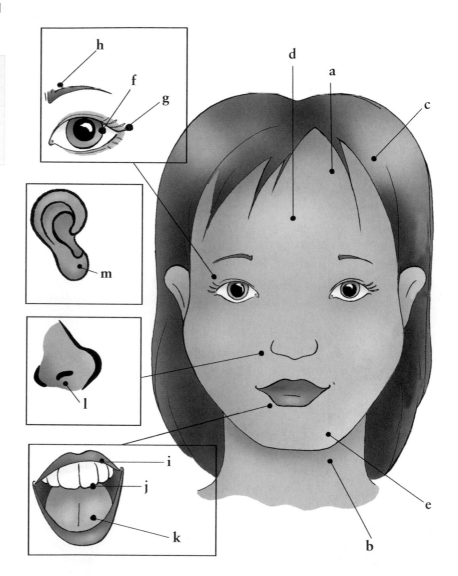

3 **In pairs What part(s) of your head and face do you use to do these things?**

a smile	g hear
b speak	h listen to music
c laugh	i see
d wink	j smell
e blink	k taste
f think	

Reading: a good night's sleep

4 **In pairs** Look at this picture and find all the reasons this person might have problems sleeping. Take it in turns to tell your partner.

Example: *She might be cold.*

5 **Quick reading** Read the text. Copy and complete the chart with the four things that stop people from sleeping. For each thing say why it stops people from sleeping.

Things that stop us from sleeping				
Why?				

Are you getting enough sleep?

Many doctors say today that sleep can change our health. If we want our bodies to work well, we need sleep. If people don't have enough sleep they can suffer from depression as well as illnesses such as heart disease.

The most obvious effect of not having enough sleep is to make us weaker and it makes it harder to fight illness; in other words, people who do not sleep enough are more likely to get sick or ill. Many people have sleeping problems. Studies in the USA have found that 60 percent of adults have problems sleeping a lot of the time. More than 40 percent of adults say that they feel sleepy in the daytime and that this makes their lives difficult. 20 percent say they sometimes have problems sleeping. At least 40 million people in the USA suffer from sleep problems that need treatment – because they sleep too much or too little – but very few people actually go to a doctor about their sleep problem.

So what are the things that affect sleep? Well, firstly, there's noise. If there are noises such as barking dogs, dripping taps and loud music, you'll probably find it difficult to sleep. What is interesting is that women seem to notice noise more than men, while young children do not notice noise as much as adults.

If you are sitting in a chair, you'll find it very difficult to sleep. But you will probably have no problem falling asleep if you are lying down. This is another thing that affects sleep – sleep surface. We need to be horizontal and we need to have enough space.

A third thing affecting sleep is temperature. You may have noticed that you have difficulty sleeping if it is very hot or cold. Studies have found that if the temperature is below 12°C or above 24°C, we will wake up.

Altitude too, can change the way we sleep. If you are at an altitude of over 4,000 m, you need to breathe differently because you don't have as much oxygen. It will take you about two weeks to get used to this.

So, if you want to sleep well:

• Do not do exercise before you go to bed.
• Do not drink alcohol or drinks like coffee that have caffeine.
• Do try to relax.

We hope this helps. Sleep well.

6 **Take a closer look** Read the passage on page 119 again more carefully. Complete the following sentences with the best word or phrase, 1, 2 or 3.

a Not having enough sleep
 1 can cause illness.
 2 does not change health.
 3 makes us stronger.

b The number of adults who say that they often have problems trying to fall asleep is
 1 40%.
 2 20%.
 3 60%.

c The people who notice noise most are
 1 men.
 2 women.
 3 babies.

d At high altitudes we need to breathe
 1 without oxygen.
 2 less oxygen.
 3 differently.

e Before you go to bed, you should NOT
 1 listen to relaxing music.
 2 drink coffee without caffeine.
 3 go for a two kilometre run.

7 Match the words in blue from the text in Activity 5 with these definitions.

a a gas that people need to breathe.
b completely flat, lying down.
c an illness which makes you feel very unhappy.
d to see, hear or feel something.
e given to someone who is ill to make them get better.
f something found in, for example, coffee that makes the body work faster.
g how high you are above sea level.

8 Answer these questions about yourself. Then compare your answers in groups.

a Have you ever found it difficult to go to sleep?
b What made it difficult for you to sleep?
c What did you do when you couldn't sleep?
d Have you ever stayed up all night without sleeping? How did you feel?

Study grammar: first conditional

> **Just learning:** *working it out for yourself*
> When you are reading, listening or working with language (in activities, etc), look at examples and try to work out for yourself what is happening. What are the rules? We often remember the rules better if we find the rule for ourselves. You can check the grammar charts and dictionaries later, but try and work things out by yourself first.

9 Look at these two sentences.

a If you are sitting in a chair, you'll find it very difficult to sleep.
b You will have no problem falling asleep if you are lying down.

There are two parts to each sentence called clauses. Each clause has a complete verb.

What verb tense is used in the *if* clause?

What verb tense is used in the other clause?

In the *if* clause, when we think it is probable that the action will happen, the verb is in a present tense. This is usually called the 'First Conditional'.

For example: **If you study hard**, you'll pass the test.

Here we believe the person will probably study hard.

→ see 3B in the Mini-grammar

How do you say sentences a and b above in your language?

10 Match the two parts of these sentences.

a If it rains on Saturday,	1 we'll come to the party.
b I'll be really happy if	2 you do vigorous exercise before you go to bed.
c If the children are feeling better,	3 you'll have no problem falling asleep.
d If there are noises,	4 we'll stay at home.
e If you are lying down,	5 if you don't finish your homework.
f It will wake you up	6 my cold is gone by tomorrow.
g You won't be able to sleep if	7 if the temperature goes above 24°C.
h I won't take you to the movie	8 you'll find it difficult to sleep.

11 Complete the following sentences with the verb in brackets in the correct tense.

  a If you .... (not lie down), you .... (not be able to) sleep.
  b Your leg .... (get) better if you .... (rest).
  c If you .... (study) hard, you .... (pass) the test.
  d You .... (feel) better if you .... (drink) more water every day.
  e Your heart .... (not get) stronger if you .... (not exercise) more.
  f If I .... (eat) more calcium, ... my bones .... (get) stronger?
  g You'll .... (catch) a cold if you .... (go out) in this rain.
  h .... you .... (help) me with my homework if I .... (wash) the dishes?
  i If you .... (listen to) that loud music, you .... (hurt) your ears.
  j .... she .... (go) on holiday if she .... (not finish) the report?

12 Complete these sentences about yourself.

  a If it rains this weekend, ...
  b I'll do some exercise if ...
  c If I pass this English course, ...
  d If I ever win a lot of money, ...

  Now compare them with a partner.

Speaking: your health

13 In pairs Take turns to ask and answer these questions with your partner.

	yes	no	sometimes
1 Do you sleep at least eight hours every night?			
2 Are those hours the same hours every night?			
3 Do you eat a balanced diet?			
4 Do you make sure physical activities are part of your daily routine?			
5 Do you drink at least two litres of clean drinking water every day?			

Now go to Activity 34 in the Activity Bank on page 143. Count your partner's score and read the explanations.

14 In groups Use your answers and the information in Activity 34 in the Activity Bank to talk about the things you can do differently.

Example: STUDENT A: I go to bed at 11.30 and I get up at 6 am.

STUDENT B: If you go to bed at 10 pm every night, you'll get eight hours sleep.

Writing: ordering important ideas

15 Which of these things do you think are important for good health? Copy and complete the chart with your order.

	My order	Marco's order
a enough sleep		
b good food		
c hobbies		
d friends		
e plenty of money		
f regular medical check-ups		
g people who care about you		
h a nice place to live		
i regular exercise		
j interesting work		

Compare with a partner.

16 Read this essay written by Marco. What order do you think he would have for the things in Activity 15? Complete the chart.

If you want to stay healthy, there are many things that you can do. The first one is to eat and sleep well. I try to sleep at least 8 hours every night and I try to eat a balanced diet. I go to see a doctor once a year for a check-up and I exercise twice a week.

It is also good for your health if you have good friends and people who care about you. You need to have people to go out with and things that interest you. If you have hobbies, this will also help you to have a healthy lifestyle.

Where you live and where you work are also important to your lifestyle. If you have a good job and a comfortable home, you will stay healthy. I am a student of medicine and I live with two friends in a nice house. This helps me a lot.

The least important thing for good health is having a lot of money. If you have a lot of money, this won't stop you from getting sick, but of course it helps you to have a more comfortable life. There are many times that I can't afford to buy the things that I want, but because I have the other things, I don't really mind.

Are Marco's most important ideas at the beginning or at the end?

17 Use your order in Activity 15 to write your own ideas about what a healthy lifestyle is.

Start with the most important things and put the least important things at the end.

Share your writing with a partner.

Listening: it's all in the eyes

18 Look at this photo of the eyes. What do you think this person is thinking?

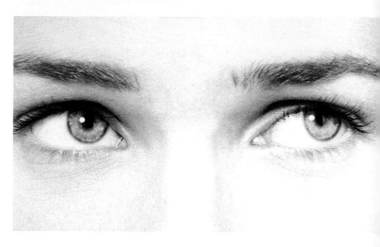

Give instructions to your classmates. Do they look in the right way?

1 look down and to the left
2 look directly left
3 look up and to the left
4 look directly right
5 look up and to the right
6 look down and to the right

19 Listen to Track 66 and answer these questions. Write Tricia (T) or Marty (M).

Who...

a tries to remember the face of a childhood friend?

b read an article about brain research and eye movement?

c says people's eyes move in different directions when they think about different things?

d can't stop looking into people's eyes?

20 Listen to Track 66 again and match the position of the eyes (numbers 1 – 6) in Activity 18 to what you are doing in your head. The first one is done for you.

a remembering an image   3 (looking up and to the left)

b inventing an image

c remembering a sound

d imagining a sound

e talking to yourself

f having feelings

21 In Marty's article, which way does it say you will look when you think about:

a a time when you felt scared?

b the sound of a big dog barking?

c the sound of your mother's voice?

d the face of a person you know?

e a picture of a high mountain?

f how you are going to solve a problem?

In pairs Take turns to think about these things and watch each other's eyes to see where they move.

Study functions: talking about similarities and differences

22 Listen to Track 67 and complete the dialogue with one of the words below.

too	so	either	neither

CHARLES: I've just started going to a new gym.

MARTINA: Oh, really? Me (**a**) .... Which gym?

CHARLES: It's called 'Get Fit'.

MARTINA: That's my gym (**b**) .... I love it.

CHARLES: (**c**) .... do I. But I don't like the trainer.

MARTINA: (**d**) .... do I. He's unfriendly, but I feel great.

CHARLES: I don't. I've only been twice.

MARTINA: (**e**) .... have I. I just don't have the time.

CHARLES: (**f**) .... do I. I'm really busy at work.

MARTINA: (**g**) .... am I. I can't go to the gym today.

CHARLES: I can't go (**h**) .... I have to work late.

MARTINA: I need more time off. I have to talk to my boss.

CHARLES: (**i**) .... do I! If we want to get healthy, we'll need to go to the gym more than once a week!

23 Are these things true for Charles (C) or Martina (M) or both (B) of them?

a She / he has just started a new gym.

b Her / his new gym is called 'Get Fit'.

c She / he doesn't like the trainer.

d She / he feels great.

e She / he has been to the gym twice.

f She / he doesn't have enough time to go to the gym.

g She / he is really busy at work.

h She / he can't go to the gym today.

i She / he needs to talk to her / his boss.

24 Complete this table with the different ways of talking about similarities.

affirmative	negative
I love my gym. .... do I. I do, ... Me.................... .	I don't do much exercise. .... do I. I don't, ...
I'm very healthy. .... am I. I am, ... Me	I'm not very fit. .... am I. I'm not, ...

25 **In pairs** How similar are we?

Student A: go to Activity 21 in the Activity Bank on page 139.

Student B: go to Activity 36 in the Activity Bank on page 144.

26 **Answer these questions about yourself.**

Where do you live?

Why are you studying English?

Do you have brothers and sisters?

What do you do?

What are your hobbies?

Compare your answers with a partner and make comments on the similarities and differences in your lives.

Pronunciation: same word, different pronunciation

27 Listen to Track 68. What do you notice about the pronunciation of either and neither?

28 Listen to Track 69. Which pronunciation do you hear?

> /aɪ/ – like *eye*   /iː/ – like *we*
>
> **a** I don't exercise often, either.
> **b** Neither do I.
> **c** Gemma isn't very fit, either.
> **d** Neither has Martin been to the new hospital.
> **e** Jessica hasn't been to the gym, either.
> **f** She won't be there, either.

Practise saying the sentences using the two different pronunciations of either and neither.

29 **Look at these words that also have two different pronunciations:**

   a room   **b** garage   **c** new

What are the different ways to pronounce them?

Note: People often ask 'Which is the correct pronunciation?' The answer is 'Neither!' Different people say the words differently. That's all.

Study grammar: first conditional and zero conditional

30 Read sentences 1 and 2.

  1 If I exercise too much, I'll get out of breath.

  2 If I exercise too much, I get out of breath.

Say which one tells you about:

a something that is always true?
b something that is possible or probable?

31 Read these sentences. Write T (true) if they tell you about something that is always true, or P (possible / probable) if they tell you about something that is possible or probable in the future.

a If you don't lie down, you won't fall asleep.

b If you are at an altitude of over 4,000 feet, you need to breathe differently.

c I always find it difficult to sleep if I drink coffee before I go to bed.

d If you drink that coffee, you won't be able to get to sleep.

e If you melt ice, it becomes water.

f If you want some dessert, you'll have to eat your dinner.

g If he doesn't study harder, he won't pass his exam.

Where might you see or hear these sentences?

32 Which of the sentences in Activity 31 have:

a the present simple in the *if* clause and the future simple in the other part of the sentence? (first conditional)

b the present simple in both clauses? (zero conditional)

→ see 3A and 3B in the Mini-grammar

33 Match the two parts of these sentences.

a If you don't get enough sleep,	1 I feel sick, because I'm allergic to them.
b You won't be able to do well in your exam	2 you sleep to the sound of water.
c If I eat mushrooms,	3 you'll feel tired for your exam.
d You always get tired	4 if you don't eat properly.
e If you live near a river,	5 it expands (gets bigger).
f If metal is heated,	6 if you run more than five miles.

34 Complete these sentences about yourself.

a If I eat too much …
b If I don't get enough sleep …
c If I study hard for this course …
d If it rains this weekend …

Compare with a partner. Which sentences were in the first conditional and which were in the zero conditional? Why?

UNIT 16
Weird and wonderful

Vocabulary: from strange to amazing

1 Read these paragraphs and put the words in blue into the word map.

This is a strange creature with two creepy eyes and four very scary claws. Its legs are odd and it is very unusual for an animal to have only three legs. Altogether it looks rather weird and unbelievable.

This is a wonderful car which looks a little funny, because it only has three wheels, but it has an incredible shape. The front of the car looks fantastic and it is a great colour – I love turquoise. It's an amazing car which can go very fast.

'weird and wonderful' words

words to describe things that frighten you	words to describe things that are unusual	words to describe things that are good

Do you know any other words that can go in this word map?

2 Complete these sentences with a suitable word from Activity 1.

a I've just seen a .... movie. It's a comedy and I laughed a lot.

b That woman is very .... She wears strange clothes and reads poetry on the bus.

c What a .... sports car. Does it go very fast?

d I don't like to be at home alone at night. I find it ....

e They say there are ghosts in that house. It's a .... place.

f This shop only sells dolls and gardening tools. What a .... shop!

g My grandfather likes to eat banana sandwiches. He's a little ....

h Did you see that .... bird? It only has one leg and one eye.

i What a .... digital camera! The pictures are so clear.

3 Which of the words in blue in Activity 1 could you use to describe these things?

a a creature with four hands

b a person who never talks to other people

c a machine to travel in time

d a cemetery where dead people are buried

e a house that nobody has lived in for twenty years

f a space ship

g a car

h a movie poster for a horror film

4 In pairs Draw a picture of something weird and/or wonderful. Give it to another pair and write a paragraph about the picture they give you. Read their paragraph about your drawing. Do you agree with the words they have used?

Study functions: paying attention

5 Look at these pictures carefully. Then listen to Track 70 and put the pictures a – f in order.

6 Listen to Track 70 again and check which of the words and expressions below you hear the listener use.

Yeah?	That's funny.
What happened next?	Right.
Really?	That's impossible!
Uh-huh.	Wow!
Then what happened?	And?
What did she say?	That's weird.
What?	That's strange.
How weird!	I see.

7 Copy the table below. Write all the words and expressions in the appropriate sections.

Things to show the speaker that you are paying attention	Uh-huh.
Asking questions	
Reacting to what the speaker says	

8 **In pairs** Using the pictures, take turns to tell the story to your partner. If you are the listener, use the words and expressions from Activity 6 to show that you are listening.

9 Think of a scary or unusual experience that happened to you, or someone you know. Note down the main points of the story.

In groups of three One is the story-teller, the others are listeners. Take it in turns.

Story teller, tell your story. Make sure the listeners stay interested.
Listeners, show that you are listening carefully and paying attention. Use the words and phrases in Activity 6.

Example: STUDENT A: So, I was at home, by myself ...

STUDENTS B AND C: Uh-huh ...

Reading: Burning Man

10 In pairs Look at this poster and answer the questions.

Are you looking for something different?

Come to **Burning Man**

Come and experience art and survival in the desert for one week.

August 29th – September 5th
Tickets $250

a Would you like to go to this event?
Why, or why not?
b Look at these questions that people ask before they go to Burning Man. What do you think the answers will be?

1 How do you get there?
2 What is Burning Man?
3 Why is it called 'Burning Man'?
4 What is there to do at Burning Man?
5 What's the weather like?
6 What does the place look like?
7 What happens when Burning Man is over?
8 What should I bring?

11 Quick reading Match the questions from Activity 10 to the right answers.

Every year for one week about 25,000 people go to the Nevada desert from around the world to an event which is called Burning Man. A 'city' is built in the middle of the Black Rock Desert. They call this city Black Rock City. They spend the week living together in the city and making art while they are there.

Before you think about going to Burning Man, read these Frequently Asked Questions (FAQs) to get an idea of what Burning Man is. It could be just right for you.

FAQs

Q. (a) ....
A. Burning Man is an experiment in living with other people. If you want to really understand Burning Man, you have to try it.

Q. (b) ....
A. You can drive to the Black Rock Desert in your car and camp, or you can come in a camper van. Many people come in an art car decorated especially for the occasion, like this one.

Q. (c) ....
A. Black Rock City is organised as two thirds (2/3) of a circle. 'The Man' is put in the centre.

Q. (d) ....
A. Water, food and shelter (a tent or other place to sleep) are the things that you must bring with you so that you can survive. Everything else you bring is up to you. Many people bring toys or costumes to play and to make art.

Q. (e) ....

A. The weather in late August/early September is usually warm, but it can be really cold. People at Burning Man have had many evenings below 40°F (4°C) and daytime temperatures over 100°F (38°C).

Q. (f) ....

A. The first thing to do is participate. You are not there to watch, you are there to make art and live in a community. Nobody at Burning Man is a spectator; you're there to build your own new world. Use your imagination.
And … you're there to survive. You have to drink water all the time and you have to cover yourself in sunblock because the sun is very strong. Remember, you cannot buy anything at Black Rock City except coffee and ice.

Q. (g) ....

A. The Man is a huge 75 ft (20m) high piece of art. It is at the centre of the city and it is the heart of this event. On Saturday night, at the end of a week, the Man is burnt.

Q. (h) ....

A. You leave as you came. When you go from Burning Man, you leave no trace. Everything you built, you take apart and take it with you. The rubbish that you made leaves with you and the Black Rock Desert returns to its perfect condition. There are volunteers who stay for weeks to clean up the desert.
But you take the world you built with you. When you have experienced Burning Man your world will change – forever.

12 Take a closer look Who or What:

a is Black Rock City?
b is the best way to understand Burning Man?
c is an art car?
d is organised to look like part of a circle?
e are the things that you must bring to the event?
f are the maximum and minimum temperatures?
g can participate in the event?
h can you buy at Burning Man?
i is 'the Man'?
j happens after the event is over?

13 Use these words and phrases from the text to complete the sentences.

> trace spectators camper van participate experiment
> sunblock shelter it's up to you survive

a My parents are going to travel through Europe in their new ...., so they won't need to stay in hotels.
b Scientists and researchers often do an .... to find out some new information.
c It was raining and very cold so we needed .... for the night – a place to stay.
d Would you like to .... in the competition? If you win, the prize is a trip to New York.
e Where do you want to go for dinner? It's your birthday so .... You can make the decision.
f When we arrived at the stadium there were 50,000 .... waiting for the match to begin.
g I looked for my dog everywhere, but there was no .... of her anywhere. Not a thing.
h It's impossible for people to .... on the moon, because there is no oxygen.
i If you sit on the beach you must wear ...., so that your skin is not hurt.

14 Noticing grammar: passive voice

Look at the orange sentences in the text. Match each sentence here with the sentence from the text that means the same.

The people at Burning Man burn 'the Man'.
The people who go to Burning Man build a city.
The people who organise the event put 'the Man' in the centre.

Identify the subject, verb and object in each of these sentences and from those in the text.

→ see 7 in the Mini-grammar

15 In groups Would you like to go to Burning Man? Why, or why not? What would you rather do instead?

Study grammar: review of present, past and future tenses

....

16 Match the sentences that mean the same thing.

Active voice	Tense	Passive voice	Tense
a They burn the Man.		1 The Man was burnt.	
b They burnt the Man.		2 The Man will be burnt.	
c They will burn the Man.		3 The Man is burnt.	

What tense is each sentence?

Choose the best passive sentence from the table above to complete each of these short texts.

a It's very exciting to be here at Burning Man. I can't wait until Saturday, because .... I really want to see that.
b There are a few things you should know about Burning Man. It lasts for one week and .... on the last day.
c We had a great time at Burning Man. We stayed all week and .... on the last day. Then we left on Sunday.

17 Match each sentence with the explanation of its meaning.

Explanations	Sentences
a a repeated action or habit in the present	1 Any plans for tomorrow? Yes, I'm going to do some housework at last.
b a prediction about the future	2 It gets darker at night.
c an interrupted action in the past	3 Have you seen this movie yet? It's wonderful.
d something that was in progress in the past	4 We were watching TV last night when my aunt called from Australia.
e a completed past action	5 The show is about a woman who lives in France.
f connects the present and the past	6 We used to go to the movies once a week. Now it's impossible.
g a general fact which is true	7 You have to see that play. You'll love it!
h an unplanned decision	8 Every day he eats lunch at Harry's restaurant.
i something in progress at the moment	9 I'm taking dance classes at the moment.
j describes what happens in a film, book, programme or story	10 The sun was shining as she walked through the park.
k a plan	11 You say the number and I'll write it down.
l a habit in the past	12 He passed the test.

18 Match the letters/numbers in Activity 17 with the following verb tenses. The first one is done for you.

going to k/1
Used to + verb
Present simple
Past continuous
Present continuous
Present perfect
Past simple
Future simple

➔ see 4, 8 and 10 in the Mini-grammar

19 Write one true sentence and one false sentence to answer each one of these questions.

a Name something you used to do as a child that you don't do now.
b What were you doing yesterday at 2 pm?
c Have you ever seen an unusual animal?

Show your partner your answers. Ask each other questions to find out which is the false sentence.

20 Write true sentences about yourself.

a What are you going to do this weekend?
b Who do you think will win the next soccer/football World Cup?
c Where are you going for your next holiday?
d What will you do when you finish studying English?

Interview your partner about their answers. You must ask at least two questions about their answers.

Listening: Unidentified Flying Objects

Just learning: *telling stories again*

In our lives we tell and re-tell stories that we have read and heard (or experienced) all the time. It's important. But re-telling is good for learners too! It helps you to remember words and grammar better. The more you re-tell a story the more you remember! Here are a few tips to help you re-tell stories in Activity 23.

1. Use the comprehension questions and answers to help you to talk about the main ideas. For example, using question one, you can say: "The story took place in Trindade Islands, Brazil ..."
2. Try to use the new vocabulary that you learned. Using it will help you to remember it.

21 Look at these two photos. What do they show? Do you believe the photographs are real?

22 Form two groups. Group A listens to Track 71 and Group B listens to Track 72. Choose the correct answer according to what you hear.

a Where did the story take place?
  1 Trindade Islands, Brazil   2 Harvard University, USA
  3 Bentwaters, England
b When did the story take place?
  1 December 1st 1957   2 December 27th 1980
  3 January 16th 1958
c What did people see first?
  1 unusual lights   2 discs flying very fast
  3 slow discs and lights
d How big was the object that people saw?
  1 20 feet wide and 30 feet high   2 47 feet high   3 50 feet wide
e Were there any photographs or other physical evidence?
  1 a noisy aeroplane   2 a series of 6 photographs
  3 broken trees and large holes in the ground
f What was the explanation given by people who did not believe the story?
  1 it was an aeroplane flying through fog
  2 it was the wind and complex scientific causes
  3 it was a radio station
g What do people say today?
  1 the objects moved slowly   2 the photographs are real
  3 experts cannot explain the high levels of radiation

23 **In pairs** Get together with someone from the other group. Check your answers.

Re-tell the story that you heard to your partner. Use the questions and answers from Activity 22 to help you.

Pronunciation: acronyms

Acronyms are words made up of the initial letters of other words, like UFO (Unidentified Flying Object).

24 Listen to Track 73. What's different about the way these two acronyms are pronounced?

  a Many people say they have seen a UFO.
  b The problem of AIDS is a huge one.

25 Listen to Track 74. Which acronyms do you hear?

  a I heard the report on the radio on the ....
  b I'm going to visit the .... next year.
  c Do you like bacon? Would you like a .... ?
  d The oil-producing nations have an organisation called ....
  e One of the most important parts of the .... is ....
  f How long is she going to stay in the .... ?
  g Have you seen my new .... player?

26 Practise saying the sentences with the correct pronunciation of these acronyms.

Find other acronyms and check how they are pronounced.

Study grammar: review of adjectives and prepositions, articles and quantifiers

27 **In pairs** Test yourselves. Discuss why the different options are correct or not correct.

a Paris is .... city in France.

   1 the largest   2 the larger   3 largest

b I don't want .... sugar, thank you.

   1 some   2 any   3 many

c I'd like .... boiled potatoes, please.

   1 some   2 one   3 much

d How .... apple juice do you need?

   1 many   2 any   3 much

e I just need .... apples for this apple pie.

   1 few   2 little   3 a few

f Nicole Kidman is .... than Julia Roberts.

   1 popular   2 most popular
   3 more popular

g Who is the .... singer in the world?

   1 better   2 good   3 best

h Iron is .... than feathers.

   1 heavier   2 more heavy   3 heaviest

i The building on the left is .... than the other one.

   1 more high   2 higher   3 highest

j This is .... book I've ever read.

   1 the more interesting   2 most interesting
   3 the most interesting

k Do you like .... animals

   1 the   2 a   3 ___

l I'm hungry. I'd like .... sandwich, please.

   1 the   2 a   3 ___

m I enjoyed walking .... the town yesterday.

   1 through   2 below   3 over

n I was driving .... a street near my house, looking at the flowers, when I saw a strange animal.

   1 into   2 along   3 inside

Compare your answers with another pair. Look back at Units 1, 2, 5 and 14 to check your answers. Explain why the answers are right or wrong.

28 Now write five test sentences with your partner. Try them on another pair.

→ see 1, 2, 6 and 9 in the Mini-grammar

Speaking: phone call

29 Read these paragraphs and answer the questions.

a Why did Andy use to hate to be alone when he was a child?

b Who was the man who called him in 1985?

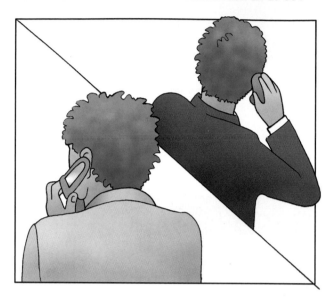

All his life, Andy Jackson hated to be alone. As a child, he always wanted someone to stay the night at his house. As a young man, he had several different friends. He always felt that he was not complete – there was something missing from his life.

That ended on Sept. 23, 1985, when the telephone rang and a voice said, "You don't know me, and this is a strange question, but when were you born?" Andy thought it was odd, but gave the answer. "Well, here's an even stranger question for you: Were you adopted?" Andy said yes. "Hi," the stranger said. "I'm your twin brother."

Andy did not know that he had a brother. When they were born they were given to two different couples. Andy discovered that his brother's name was Kevin and soon found that there were many similarities and differences between them.

Student A: go to Activity 22 in the Activity Bank page 139.

Student B: go to Activity 37 in the Activity Bank page 144.

Continue the telephone conversation between Andy and Kevin. Find all the similarities and differences between them.

Writing: making your story interesting

30 Read these two ways of telling the same story. A is a complete story and B is the beginning of the same story.

A

One day, Robert Barnes was in his garden and he was planting flowers. He heard a voice behind him. The voice said "Leave us alone". He turned around. There was no one there. He looked into the history of the house and found that the house had a long history. Many bad things happened there.

B

Last week I was at home in my garden. It was a beautiful day and I decided to plant some flowers. As I was digging a hole, I felt the air go cold and the hairs on my arms stood up. Suddenly I had the feeling that I was not alone ...

31 **In pairs** What are the differences between the two ways of telling the story? Copy and use this table.

	A	B
Who tells the story?		
How does the writer describe the scene?		
How are feelings described?		
Does the writer use a lot of detail?		

32 **In pairs** Imagine you are Robert Barnes. Complete story B in your own words. Try to make your story as interesting and exciting as possible. Talk about your feelings and the events so that the reader feels more interested in the story.

Read your stories to other pairs and decide which one is the most interesting.

33 Now write another story:

EITHER:

Write a true story about something weird or wonderful that has happened to you.

OR

Imagine you are one of the people in the Trindade or Bentwaters stories (Activity 22) and write about seeing a UFO.

Activity bank

1 [Unit 1]

Ask B questions about their country. Copy and complete the chart.

Where it is:
Capital:
Languages:
Most popular sports:
Interesting information:

Example: *What's interesting about your country?*

Can you guess B's country?

Read the information about the country below and answer B's questions. DO NOT SAY the name of the country. Can B guess the name of the country and find it on the map?

> Name: New Zealand
> Where it is: In the Pacific Ocean. It has two islands.
> Capital: Wellington
> Languages: English, Maori
> Most popular sports: rugby, water sports, cricket
> Interesting information: There are many high mountains and several volcanoes - some still active.
> The Maori are the indigenous people of New Zealand (they were there first and then the British arrived).

2 [Unit 2]

a Read the joke to yourself. The punch line is in italics.
b Tell the joke to your partner. Does he/she understand it? Does he/she think it is funny?

> A boy goes to school with a huge lump in his head. 'James,' said the teacher. 'What happened to your head?'
> 'A tomato fell on it, Sir.'
> 'A tomato!' said the teacher, very surprised. 'A very big tomato!'
> 'No. Sir,' said James. '*It was small but it was in a tin.*'

3 [Unit 3]

You want to watch a live pop concert. It is on Channel 3. It's from 6.00 to 8.00.

a When is your programme? Look at the TV guide on page 29.
b In your group, find the best choice for everyone to watch.

4 [Unit 4]

5 [Unit 3]

You really want to watch the next episode of *Home and Away*, your favourite Australian soap. Today we find out Danny's terrible secret. It's a very important episode! *Home and Away* is from 6.00 to 6.30.

a When is your programme? Look at the TV guide on page 29.
b In your group, find the best choice for everyone to watch.

6 [Unit 5]

Find as many differences between your picture and Student A's picture as possible.

Example: Is the limousine in front of the Just Films building?

7 [Unit 6]

Read the situation and answer the questions to make up a story. Tell the story to your partner.

You were on the bus. You found a piece of paper. It looked important so you picked it up.

• What was it?
A lottery ticket? A phone number? A bank note? A cheque?

• What did you do with it?
Did you give it to somebody? Did you keep it? Did you throw it away again?

• What happened in the end?
You don't know if the owner found his/her paper.

• How do you feel about what happened?
Are you worried about what you did? Do you think you made the right decision? Do you feel sorry about what you did?

Now listen to your partner's story and react to it. Use expressions from the chart in Activity 29 on page 52.

8 [Unit 3]

You are doing a project about the Far East. Tonight, on Channel 2, there is a documentary about Japan. You think it is probably really useful for your project.

a When is your programme? Look at the TV guide on page 29.
b In your group, find the best choice for everyone to watch.

9 [Unit 6]

Mrs Hall is about 100 years old.

Mrs Hall used to watch silent films when she was a child – movies with sound (talkies) started in 1927. Cars became more common from 1907. The telephone began in the 1880s. Television began in the 1930s but television sets were expensive and not many people had them.

10 [Unit 7]

a You won this voucher for a hang-gliding lesson for two. Invite your partner to go with you.

b Now listen to B's invitation. Accept or reject it giving him/her as many reasons as you can for your decision.

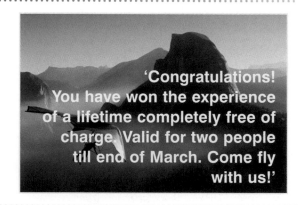

'Congratulations! You have won the experience of a lifetime completely free of charge. Valid for two people till end of March. Come fly with us!'

11 [Unit 7]

Science and Nature
a a reptile expert
b the part of the brain that stores things for a long time
c something that gives you stress

Sports and Leisure
a a Brazilian activity
b you sit on it and bounce
c on a river

Geography
a Scotland
b Kingston
c Canada

Entertainment
a Australia
b Homer, Marge, Bart, Maggie, Lisa, Abraham, Snowball, etc.
c a television or radio drama that never ends

12 [Unit 8]

At 10 o'clock last night you were at the cinema with your new boyfriend/girlfriend (but you don't want people to know). You dislike mice and you think animal experiments are necessary.

13 [Unit 14]

Building 1 is the opera house in Santa Cruz, Tenerife (in the Canary Islands).
Building 2 is the Selfridges department store in Birmingham, England.
Building 3 is the Deep, in Hull, England. This is a visitor centre where people look at exhibitions about life under the sea.
Building 4 is the Modern Art Centre in Cincinnati, USA.

14 [Unit 8]

At 10 o'clock last night you were visiting a friend (Student D). You watched TV together.
You secretly disagree with animal experiments. You think it is wrong, so you are happy the mice escaped.

15 [Unit 9]

Read the text about your new mobile phone. Make a list of what you can do with it.

Example: I can take photos and send them to friends.

Congratulations! You now have the best mobile phone on the market. It is a multimedia centre in one machine.
- Take photos and send them to your friends.
- Make a video and share it with friends. Play your favourite game.
- Send emails wherever you are.
- Talk to friends and watch them on the screen.
- Play your favourite music.
- You can make normal calls, too.
- Leave a picture or video message.

Can your partner do the same things as you? Ask questions.

Example: YOU: Can you take photos and send them to friends?
           YOUR PARTNER: Yes, I can/No, I can't.

16 [Unit 12]

You want to invite Jim Garcia.

Profession	Will talk about	Reasons to invite him
Firefighter	Being a firefighter: what you have to do, personal experiences	Interesting topic Exciting experiences Good topic for all types of people

1 You must introduce the person you would like to invite and give reasons why you think he would be the best person to invite.

Example: I'd like to invite Jim Garcia. He's a 28 year-old firefighter. He'll talk about ...

2 Listen carefully to the chairperson and follow instructions.

17 [Unit 8]

At 10 o'clock last night you went into the lab and let the mice escape. Animal experiments make you very angry. You love all animals and wanted to save the mice. You are proud you saved the mice but you don't want any trouble. You were alone. You need to make up an excuse!

18 [Unit 13]

Answer the interviewer's questions as if you are Gemma, Maria and Gerry. Invent any information that is not in the picture.

Example: INTERVIEWER: Gemma, what are you going to do when you leave school?

GEMMA (YOU): I'm going to study ...

Now, you are the interviewer. Ask Martin, Jeff and Christy about their future plans.

Example: INTERVIEWER (YOU): Martin, what are you going to do when you leave school?

MARTIN: I'm going to ...

19 [Unit 14]

Facts and figures

The Great Wall of China
People have different opinions about the length of the Great Wall of China. Some people say it is about 2,400 km (about 1,500 miles) long, but other people look at the beginning and end of the different 'walls' that make up the one big wall and say that it is 6,400 km (4,000 miles), or even longer.

The Matterhorn
The Matterhorn, one of Switzerland's most beautiful mountains, is 4,478 metres high.

The Petronas Towers
The Petronas Towers, built in 1998, are 452 metres tall (1,483 feet), and have 88 storeys.

The Mississippi River
The total length of the Mississippi is 3,779 km (2,348 miles). At its beginning, it is between 20-30 feet wide, the narrowest stretch for its entire length. But when it gets to Lake Onalaska it is 4 miles wide. In New Orleans it is 200 feet deep.

The Pacific Ocean
The Pacific Ocean is 4,280 metres deep (14,040 feet). The Mariana Trench (near Guam) is 11,033 metres deep (36,198 feet) – the deepest water in the world.

The 9th of July Avenue
The Avenida 9 de Julio (9th of July Avenue) in Buenos Aires has 16 lanes of traffic at its widest point.

The Witswatersrand Gold Mine
The Witswatersrand gold mine has a main shaft (tunnel down into the earth) which is 2,993 metres deep.

The River Thames
The River Thames is about 344 kilometres (215 miles) long.

20 [Unit 12]

You want to invite Jonathan Singh.

Profession	Will talk about	Reasons to invite him
Medical biologist	Finding cures for diseases	Very important topic Relevant to everyone in the world Interesting and useful language

1 You must introduce the person you would like to invite and give reasons why you think he would be the best person to invite.

Example: I want to invite Jonathan Singh. He's a medical biologist and he's 33 years old.

2 Listen carefully to the chairperson and follow the instructions.

21 [Unit 15]

Look at the information.

Name: Max Lee
Place of work: Bancroft Hospital
Job: Children's doctor
Works with: Children
Family: Married with no children
Home: London
Likes: skiing and golf
Dislikes: watching TV and football

You are Max. You meet Harry (Student B) at a party. Have a conversation and make comments about your similarities and differences (like the picture).

22 [Unit 16]

You are Andy. Use this information about Andy to answer the questions that Kevin asks you.
Ask Kevin questions. You may invent any information that is not in the table:

Occupation	Manager of a supermarket
Family	Married for ten years to Jane (cashier), three children (Brad 8, Molly 4, Johnny 3 years old)
Education	Did not go to university or college – left school at age 18.
Personality	Calm, relaxed
Home	A large house about 70 miles from Los Angeles, California

Example: ANDY: So, Kevin, what do you do?
KEVIN: I'm the manager of a bookstore. What about you?
ANDY: I'm a manager too.

23 [UNIT 1]

Read the information about the country below and answer A's questions. DO NOT SAY the name of the country. Can A guess the name of the country and find it on the map?

Name: South Africa
Where it is: the most southerly part of Africa
Capital: Two – Pretoria and Cape Town
Languages: Afrikaans, English, Zulu and others
Most popular sports: rugby, cricket, water sports, like surfing
Interesting information: It is richer than other African countries. There are many modern cities. 18 percent of the population is white, 70 percent is black.

Ask A questions about their country. Copy and complete the chart.

Where it is:	
Capital:	
Languages:	
Most popular sports:	
Interesting information:	

Example: What's interesting about your country?
Can you guess A's country?

24 [Unit 2]

a Read the joke to yourself. The punch line is in italics.
b Tell the joke to your partner. Does he/she understand it? Does he/she think it is funny?

A man wanted to buy a Rolls Royce all his life. For years and years he saved all his money. Finally, one day he went to buy his Rolls Royce. He gave all the money to the salesman. The salesman counted it. 'I'm sorry, sir,' he said, 'but you need twenty more pence.'
The man ran to the street and went up to a policeman. 'Excuse me,' he said, 'can you give me 20p? I want to buy a Rolls Royce.'
'That's OK,' said the policeman. 'Here's 40p –get one for me too.'

25 [Unit 3]

You don't care what you watch as long as it is not news or sports. You think they're boring.

a Look at the TV guide on page 29.
b In your group, find the best choice for everyone to watch.

26 [Unit 6]

Read the situation and answer the questions to make up a story. Tell the story to your partner.

You had a long day and you needed to relax. You decided to go for a walk. In the street you saw a famous person. He/she asked you a question.

- What question did the person ask you?
  Did he/she ask you for directions? Did he/she ask you for your phone number? Did he/she ask your name? Did he/she want to borrow your mobile phone?

- What did you do?
  Did you answer the question correctly? Did you lie? Did you help?

- What happened in the end?
  Did you have a conversation? Did the person give you something? Did he/she just say 'thank you'?

Now listen to your partner's story and react to it. Use expressions from the chart in Activity 29 on page 52.

27 [Unit 7]

a Listen to A's invitation. Accept or reject it giving him/her as many reasons as you can for your decision.

b You've won this voucher for a Capoeira lesson for two. Invite your partner to go with you.

'Congratulations! You have won a free introduction to Capoeira, Brazil's most exciting export. Valid for two people till end of March. Bring a friend and share the experience!'

28 [Unit 3]

You are mad about football. Tonight is the football World Cup Final! It is showing on Channel 1.
a When is your programme? Look at the TV guide on page 29.
b In your group, find the best choice for everyone to watch.

29 [Unit 8]

At 10 o'clock last night you were at home. You are not interested in science. You hate small animals like mice and rats. You think they are dirty. You were not feeling very well and a friend (Student E) was visiting you. You watched TV together.

30 [Unit 12]

You want to invite Claudia Barker.

Profession	Will talk about	Reasons to invite her
Student and environmental volunteer	How to save the world, protecting the environment	Young, interesting Important information for everyone Good stories about her own experiences

1 You must introduce the person you would like to invite and give reasons why you think she would be the best person to invite.

Example: I'd like to invite Claudia Barker. She's an environmental volunteer.

2 Listen carefully to the chairperson and follow instructions.

31 [Unit 9]

Read the text about your new mobile phone. Make a list what you can do with it.

Example: I can take photos and send them to friends.

Congratulations! You now have one of the best mobile phones on the market.
* Take photos and send them to friends.
* Make calls without holding your phone.
* Leave photo messages.
* Send emails from anywhere and whenever you want.
* Play a computer game.
* You can make normal calls too!

Can your partner do the same things as you? Ask questions.

Example: YOU: Can you take photos and send them to friends?
YOUR PARTNER: Yes, I can/ No, I can't.

32 [Unit 8]

You are the detective. You need to ask the other students questions like these:

– How do you feel about animal experiments?
– Where were you last night at 10 o'clock?
– Who were you with?
Think of more questions to ask!

33 [Unit 13]

First, you are the interviewer. Ask Gemma, Maria and Gerry about their future plans.

Example: INTERVIEWER (YOU): *Gemma, what are you going to do when you leave school?*

GEMMA: *I'm going to study ...*

Now, answer the interviewer's questions as if you are Martin, Christy and Jeff. Invent any information that is not in the picture.

Example: INTERVIEWER: *Martin, what are you going to do when you leave school?*

MARTIN (YOU): *I'm going to ...*

34 [Unit 15]

Question 1 and Question 2
yes = 2 points, no = 0 points, sometimes = 1 point
Your body needs to have a regular sleep pattern or routine. Not getting enough sleep can be bad for the body.

Question 3
yes = 2 points, no = 0 points, sometimes = 1 point
A balanced diet means you need to eat enough protein (that you can find in meat, fish, eggs and cheese) and carbohydrates (found in bread, pasta and rice). You should eat just a little fat and enough of the vitamins and minerals that your body needs.

Question 4
yes = 2 points, no = 0 points, sometimes = 1 point
You need to take a 10 minute break for every hour that you are sitting. You also need to do 20 minutes of vigorous exercise – exercise that makes you breathe faster and sweat – at least 5 times a week.

Question 5
yes = 2 points, no = 0 points, sometimes = 1 point
Coffee, alcohol and other drinks do not count as they do not help the body in the same way that water does. Remember, our bodies are 70% water.

Total score:
8 – 10 points: You have good habits and will stay healthy if you continue to eat, sleep and exercise well.
5 – 7 points: You will need to change some of your habits if you want to stay healthy. Check which things you need to change.
0 – 4 points: If you want to have good health, you will need to change your eating, sleeping and exercise habits. Look at the quiz again to see what you need to do.

35 [Unit 12]

You want to invite Brenda Morris.

Profession	Will talk about	Reasons to invite her
Clown	Magic tricks, how to juggle	Funny To learn some magic Everyone will be relaxed and laugh

1 You must introduce the person you would like to invite and give reasons why you think she would be the best person to invite.

Example: I want to invite Brenda Morris. She's a professional clown.

2 Listen carefully to the chairperson and follow instructions.

36 [Unit 15]

Look at the information.

Name: Harry Marshall
Place of work: Royal Hospital
Job: Nurse
Works with: Old people
Family: Married with no children
Home: Oxford
Likes: golf and football
Dislikes: watching TV and skiing

You are Harry. You meet Max (Student A) at a party. Have a conversation and make comments about your similarities and differences (like the picture).

Oh really. So do I. What do you do?

I work in a hospital

37 [Unit 16]

You are Kevin. Use this information about Kevin to answer the questions that Andy asks you.
Ask Andy questions. You may invent any information that is not in the table:

Occupation	Manager of a bookstore
Family	Married for three years to a police officer (Mary). Three children (twins Kevin and Susie 2, and Brad 6 months)
Education	Studied English literature at college.
Personality	Serious, ambitious
Home	A large apartment in Los Angeles, California

Example: ANDY: So, Kevin, what do you do?
      KEVIN: I'm the manager of a bookstore. What about you?
      ANDY: I'm a manager too.

38 [Unit 12]

You are the chairperson of the meeting.

1 Introduce yourself and tell the others the purpose of the meeting: to decide on a speaker to invite to your English class. Ask each person to present the person they would like to invite and to say why.
2 Now they can ask questions and discuss why their person is the best person to invite. You can ask questions too.
3 Listen carefully to what they say and, at the end, you must decide on the best person to invite to speak in your English class.